The FATHER'S GUIDE

The

FATHER'S GUIDE

Raising a Healthy Child

✦

Roger M. Barkin, M.D.

Fulcrum, Inc.
Golden, Colorado

Book Design by
JR Designs

Library of Congress
CATALOGING-IN-PUBLICATION DATA

Barkin, Roger M.
The Father's Guide

Includes Index.
1. Children—Care. 2. Children—Diseases—Treatment.
3. Child rearing. 4. Father and child. I. Title

RJ61.B2175 1988 649'.1 88-16370
ISBN 1-55591-031-9

Printed in the United States

10 9 8 7 6 5 4 3 2 1

Fulcrum, Inc.
Golden, Colorado

DEDICATION

This book for fathers, by a father, is a synthesis of knowledge gained through formal education, many years of being a pediatrician and, perhaps most importantly, from raising two boys. This book is dedicated to my mentors, my patients and my family who have taught and steered me throughout my professional and family life. My wife, Suzanne, and my children, Adam and Michael, have helped me learn and appreciate the joys of fatherhood and the wonders of sharing in the excitement of growth and development. This book is written for all men who are lucky enough to be able to actively share as a partner in parenting and to derive the joy that fatherhood permits.

Although the information and recommendations in this book are based on sound medical judgment, individual doctors necessarily take different approaches. You should always consult your doctor if your child has worrisome or complicating problems. Medical care is a series of judgments. Only your doctor can be certain that a specific plan is correct for your child. This book should be read within that context.

CONTENTS

Chapter 8: SPECIFIC ILLNESSES and PROBLEMS

FOREWORD

Although I had a career when Roger and I married and began planning a family, I did most of the parenting, as Roger was totally absorbed with the pressures, stress and excitement of medicine. When our children were ages two and four, however, years of discussion culminated in my returning to school to pursue a new career.

To achieve a reasonable balance between parenting and professional growth, we came up with one obvious solution—Roger had to assume an equal parenting role. Each of us decided to reconstruct our priorities and be flexible in determining family and household responsibilities.

This was the beginning of what we have come to understand is really two careers for fathers and mothers as they balance the joys and responsibilities of parenting with those of the workplace. For us, it has been a wonderful balance and has allowed us to grow in mutual understanding and cohesiveness as a family and as individuals. There is no question that new stresses and anxieties have developed, but there has been nothing more wonderful or gratifying than watching our children grow within the model that we envisioned. Roger has been able to share in the daily changes in our kids, their wants and desires, their aspirations and their fears. It is important to note, however, that although we are quite happy with the balance we have reached, every family reaches its own balance and by no means is our pattern right for everyone.

I am excited about this book because I sincerely believe that it fills a real void in helping you, as fathers, to approach your new role with enthusiasm, vigor, anticipation, excitement and joy. Fatherhood will clearly be the most wonderful role you ever assume.

Roger and I wish you all the joy we have had in raising our children. Relax, participate, share and mold your children within the environment that you have chosen—it will be wonderful!

Suzanne Barkin, M.D.

PREFACE

This book is for dads, particularly those of us who have assumed active careers outside of the workplace as fathers and parents. For years, joint parenting ended after we went to Lamaze classes and the delivery room. Clearly, we have extended our roles beyond that point into a complex balance between two careers—work and fatherhood. This new balance is often in response to changing priorities due to a working spouse, divorce or the death of a spouse. As fathers, our excitement, pleasure and challenge escalate as we watch our children grow and mature. We have the joy of participating in this process more intimately than any generation has in the past.

This book focuses on infancy and early childhood and will help you enjoy and feel comfortable with your children and the issues that confront you on a daily basis. It incorporates the experiences of many parents, children, doctors and nurses; however, it must necessarily be a personal statement. Through this book, I hope to give you a perspective on normal behavior and development and focus on areas of potential concern and conflict. Because it is essential for you to develop a philosophy for bringing up your own children, I present an approach that allows you to mold, evolve and define your own framework for being a father. By doing this, you can enjoy watching your children grow—the daily changes are amazing and startling. Loving your children adds to your own identity and *joie de vivre;* simultaneously it allows your children to mold their own image and self-esteem.

Being a father means you must constantly set priorities for your personal and job goals to make them both work; balancing your two careers and the time demands is imperative. Time is your most limited commodity; use it well. There are really no such things as super dads, just those who make decisions that permit the juggling of responsibilities. Paramount to defining your own role is to clarify your priorities and your particular measures of success. The more visible and quantifiable evidence, such as position, income and possessions, are difficult to discount, but must be placed in perspective with children, marriage and family. Success at home and work are not mutually exclusive, but both take dedication, commitment and hard work. As our children grow up, rarely do dads regret spending too little time at work. The regrets usually stem from spending too little time with the kids as they learned, matured and developed.

In the months ahead, you will find it essential to know how to handle common and emergency medical problems that may be encountered daily, particularly during your child's infancy. This information appears in the latter section of the book to help you understand these problems and, perhaps most importantly, to know when to call for help. As a doctor, I stress home treatment, to help you become your doctor's assistant by beginning therapy and watching for concerning changes at home. The index and the figure on the inside of the front cover will make it easier to find information on specific problems quickly.

As a pediatrician and father, I love watching my boys grow. Each week, each month and each year they are sources of pride, comfort and joy that allow our relationship to become closer. I also gain better perspective on the issues that face my wife and me as we share the pleasures of parenting on a more equal basis.

The hours, pressures and activities I have shared with my children have helped to build a bond between us that was new for me and often not available to previous generations. It has been wonderful, but each option has its costs, rewards and pleasures. For each person, it is a personal decision based on past experiences and future expectations that create a unique balance. More and more society is considering this sharing acceptable and a trend that should be supported.

To this book I bring the experience of being the father of two boys who have grown with careful nurturing and through their own strengths. Superimposed on this delightful process was my wife's return to school for further training. This decision was truly a mutual one, based upon sifting the options and understanding the implications.

Parenthood is indeed one of the most fantastic experiences we share with our children. It is my hope that this book, with its clear orientation toward fathers, will help you to feel more comfortable in your expanded role so that you may enjoy your children as much as I have. Parenting should be shared and savored. Enjoy every moment, for your children will grow up faster than anyone could anticipate. Stay involved and show interest. Feel good about who you are and make your children feel good about themselves and know how to be happy and positive.

To help bring focus to your parenting role, recollect your own childhood and your relationship with your own father. It may be helpful to write a letter to your father (you need not send it) about what you remember sharing—the sad, the happy and the troubling times should all be discussed. After you read the first few chapters of this book you may want to write a second letter (again, not to send but to put your thoughts into perspective), but this time to your children about your philosophy, your hopes and your dreams for them. Periodically, you may want to read this second letter to see if adjustments are needed along the way.

This is a book for you! As you learn more about your role as a father, please send me comments, personal experiences, useful approaches and suggestions; they will be incorporated in future editions. Through sharing, we can all become better parents and enjoy fathering even more.

Roger M. Barkin
Rose Medical Center
Denver, Colorado 80220

FATHERING within a CHANGING FAMILY

Chapter 1

HISTORICAL PERSPECTIVE

Changes in American society have produced numerous alterations in family structure. We as fathers have assumed a more coequal partnership in raising our children. This increased involvement crosses all cultural and socioeconomic classes. As fathers, we are no longer the invisible parent. Indeed, in many families, fathers have assumed a major role in shared parenting or as the primary caregiver when death or divorce has intervened in family relationships. These enormous changes in the family give us opportunities that few fathers have really had in the past.

Historically, men have been considered to have minimal child-rearing skills, a notion that has obviously proven untrue.

Stereotyping of our sociocultural and economic environment has led to distinct role identification that is no longer appropriate. We have traditionally derived our concepts of parenting from our own fathers; now, these relationships are changing in a very positive fashion. In every setting where it has been tested, men quickly acquire the skills and sensitivity necessary for nurturing. Increasingly, elementary and secondary school education is providing children with an earlier understanding of the changing role of men in society.

Even if your early exposure to infants was limited, one of the remarkable things about parenting is that you will feel a phenomenal sense of warmth and love toward your baby after birth. You will acquire tremendous sensitivity and responsiveness toward your infant's needs and communications, even if previously you were relatively passive and uninterested in infants. A unique bond will develop almost instantaneously between you and your new baby. As one new father observed, the birth of his child was similar to a "rite of passage," transforming him overnight from a 37-year-old post-pubescent adolescent into a father. Many dads remain skeptical of this process before delivery; just relax and let it happen! It will if you give the change a chance.

In many respects, being a father today is more difficult than in previous generations, but the rewards are significantly greater. Evolving attitudes toward the balance of family and work have produced a marked rethinking of roles. Mothers are no longer stereotyped as the ones raising the children and fathers as the ones having careers and being the disciplinarians. No longer is bringing home a paycheck and periodically reading a bedtime story the model for us as fathers.

From the beginning, we are intimately involved. Fathers are increasingly participating during preparation for childbirth and in the delivery room. We actively help to raise our children by changing diapers, giving bottles, going shopping and being involved in home and parenting activities on a constant basis. These changes are evident in our daily lives and are reflected in the advertising messages directed at infant products—dads changing diapers, giving baths and feeding children. We share car-pooling responsibilities, take our children to child care, go to school on parents' day, stay home when our children get sick, and take our children to the doctor for checkups. Coaching a soccer or baseball team or leading a scout troop become joint activities. Some dads become the primary caregivers, raising children either as single parents or with joint custody.

The balancing act that we as fathers, as well as our wives, have undertaken results in changed styles of parenting; many times stress increases when trying to balance the responsibilities of work and family. We all remember the times when we worked late and felt guilty about missing a family activity; the reverse has also happened when the kids wanted to do something and delayed timetables or interfered with productivity related to career and financial stability. This paradox of changing priorities faces us all on a daily basis.

A sense of sharing must pervade every aspect of raising our children. In families with working parents, the flexibility of individuals often determines which parent will actually be involved with an activity, rather than previous stereotypes and conventions. Women still assume the major responsibility for family organizational issues in most settings, with familial expectations often determining relative roles. For predominantly financial reasons, some families have reversed the traditional roles, with dad remaining at home ("house husband") and mom working.

No matter what your level of involvement, it is essential that you are allowed to become comfortable with a new sense of closeness with your children. Discussion of your evolving role will also allow your wife to comfortably assume a new role in the family. Shared parenting requires ongoing communication, openness and honesty. This is clearly a dynamic process, adapting to changes in work and home involvement over your children's early years, as well as later on when they enter day care, preschool, elementary school, etc.

Single-parent families—10 percent of which are headed by men—and those with limited maternal presence present fathers with different responsibilities. The complexities of these situations require individual perspective and reflection; the ultimate impact on your children largely depends on the level of family function prior to the divorce, separation or death, and your commitment to parenting as a priority in the complex balance between work, personal freedom and children.

The trade-offs for our families are clearly different from previous generations. Priorities represent a balance between personal and career goals. Acquisition of money is not always our paramount goal; increasingly, dads are nurturing their children while supporting and encouraging spouses to develop careers and interests beyond those of raising children. Measures of success must be individually defined; visible and quantifiable parameters must be carefully weighed against the rewards of intimately watching our children grow. It is a complex balance that each of us must personally determine.

In settings where dads are supportive, moms are more effective in both the family and the work place. Increasingly, surveys note that men find the experience of raising children to be among the most satisfying of life activities. You will certainly agree with this as you spend time with your children.

A particularly telling acknowledgment of this marked change is evident in Benjamin Spock and Michael Rothenberg's classic child-care book, *Dr. Spock's Baby and Child Care* (Pocket Books, New York). In 1968, they wrote, "Fathers should be active parents, but of course I don't mean the father should give as many bottles or change as many diapers as the mother. . . . He might make the formula on Sundays." In the 1985 edition, this changed to, "A father with a full-time job, even when the mother is staying at home—will do best by his children, his wife, and himself if he takes on half or more of the management of the children when he gets home from work and on weekends. The mother's leadership and patience will probably have worn thin by the end of the day. The children will profit from experiencing a variety of styles of leadership and control. When a father does his share as a matter of course when at home . . . it shows that he believes that this work is crucial for the welfare of the family, that it calls for judgment and skill, and that it is his responsibility as much as it is [mother's] when he is at home. This is what sons and daughters need to see in action if they are to grow up without sexist attitudes . . . The work should be done in the spirit of equal partnership." It is truly extraordinary how less than 20 years created such a contrast of expectations and advice!

UNIQUE CHARACTERISTICS OF FATHERING

As a father, you contribute uniquely to raising your children. Shared parenting improves your children's relationships with both you and your wife.

Mothers and fathers contribute in distinct ways to the cognitive development of children. Mothers tend to stimulate children by talking, showing and demonstrating new toys and activities, all combined with warmth and affection. Fathers tend to spend more of their time playing with their children and are more likely to pick up their children and engage in stimulating, physical activities such as peek-a-boo and ball toss. Fathers are less verbal and more tactile, especially with their sons. Their interactions with their daughters involve more verbal stimulation including talking, praising and complimenting. These subtle differences may encourage play that is traditionally considered sex appropriate. Fathers' expectations for daughters will probably evolve with changing values and increasing participation of women in the work place. You can help them develop self-confidence and a broader definition of "being female" by allowing them to get involved in traditional "male" activities such as fixing the car or house or throwing the football. You should also be willing to discuss sensitive issues and learn about the medical issues unique to your daughters.

The wonderfully positive impact of your involvement extends beyond intellectual development. Children growing up in households with shared parenting are more likely to develop good peer relationships and the ability to handle strange situations. They have more secure self images and are less apt to stereotype in work-related and personal roles.

Your impact on your children ultimately reflects a constellation of factors including the emotional state of you and your wife as parents, your financial security and your agreement about parenting skills and family values. Communication skills among all family members become paramount in developing shared concepts of child rearing.

STRESS in the WORKING FAMILY

Families in which mom and dad both work or are actively involved in outside activities must recognize the additional stresses that exist. Fathers who share the responsibilities of child rearing help to minimize this stress while fulfilling their desire to develop more significant roles in raising their children. This comes from a mutual understanding of the shared nature of bringing up children. When they are supportive of their wives, marital stress is decreased and the relationship functions better. While this is certainly a worthwhile and important goal, it requires commitment and hard work.

Burdens of time and priorities necessarily have an impact on the family unit. Indeed, we must constantly reach compromises between family and work. Often, work must be altered when possible to increase flexibility of hours, vacation, travel time, patterns of delegation and assumption of responsibilities. Work should not be brought home and certainly should not be the focus during family time, unless family activities and communication have already taken place.

Organization is essential to reducing stress. Several steps may be helpful:

1. Simplify your life and set priorities. You can't do everything. Compromise and be flexible when necessary;
2. Establish blocks of time without outside interruptions to spend time with your children or complete specific activities;
3. Maintain a calendar for home and personal activities and work;
4. Use waiting time effectively;
5. Schedule time for yourself;
6. Use available resources such as family, friends, work associates and outside help.

Let all members of the family assume some independence. As your children grow up, let them perform more chores. Trade-offs are constantly necessary, and you and your wife must decide which trade-offs are appropriate and possible. If financially feasible, consider hiring help for common, repetitive activities such as cutting the lawn or cleaning the house. Set new priorities for your participation in volunteer organizations. Consider omitting some activities. Maximize efficiency. Identify time-consuming activities that can be eliminated. Time is your most limited commodity; eliminating or changing patterns for routine tasks often reduces demands and therefore stress.

Individualize and adopt a shared parenting role in your family. This may mean that traditional roles are maintained and work well. However, it may also lead to a more contemporary model, with routine chores performed interchangeably by either spouse. By maintaining a sense of warmth and quality time, mom and dad are able to experience more of the nurturing experience. In single-parent families, the balance may be different and the choices more limited. Time remains a precious commodity and must be guarded and prioritized within a structure of flexibility and organization. To be successful, guidelines and decisions must be based on the values, preferences and socioeconomic circumstances of the parents rather than on traditional societal expectation.

Whatever relationship a given family adopts and evolves, the sharing and increased involvement of fathers is a model that has tremendous positive rewards for everyone and may assist in clarifying values and setting priorities. It should be encouraged, supported and nurtured in whatever way seems appropriate and feasible for you.

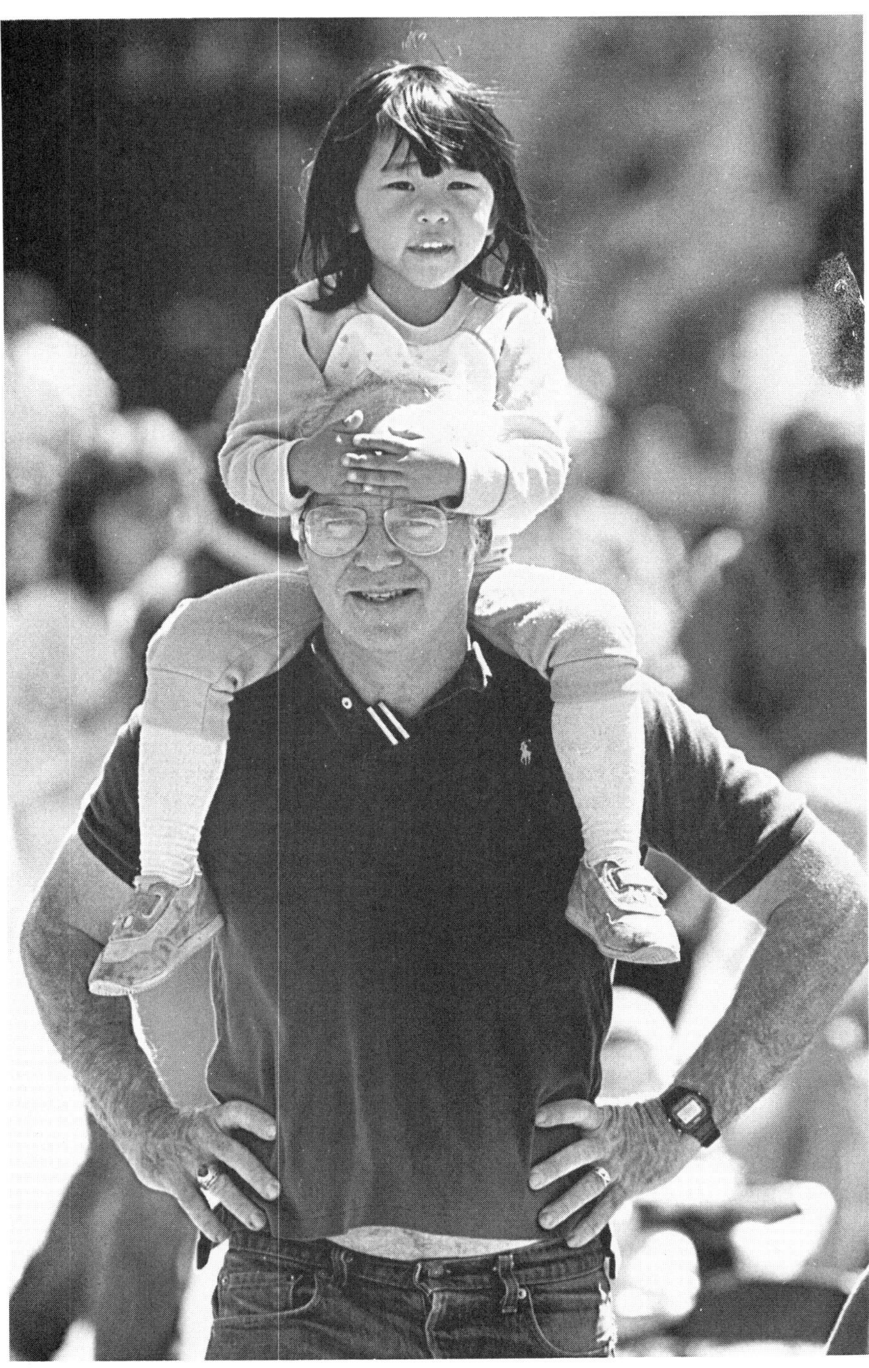

RAISING YOUR CHILDREN

Chapter 2

Child rearing largely reflects the shared values of the adults your children come in contact with—you, mom and others. To be successful, you must all reach some consensus regarding values; a consistent framework is required for your children to grow and mature. You must weigh all suggestions and recommendations within this framework to be certain that they are acceptable and consistent. You will quickly realize that there is never a shortage of advice and questions from loving relatives and friends; these too must be kept in perspective.

Throughout, your child's individuality must be appreciated, respected and enjoyed. A child develops into an independent young adult very rapidly, so enjoy and share every moment of this exciting process. Make expectations and activities appropriate for his or her ages, while being reasonable and supportive of your child's learning and growth. Allow your child to experiment and explore; risks are sometimes essential to allow for self-confidence to develop but must be monitored and reasonable. Children often model themselves after adults, so it is important to expose your child to an adult environment while actively encouraging activities with other children.

Trust yourself as a parent and provide a role model demonstrating a positive self-image that your children can draw upon. Instincts based on love and caring are usually correct; they provide the basis for synthesizing the inordinate amount of advice you will get about approaches and responsibilities of child rearing. Recognize that a father is similar to being a teacher and is perhaps the most important teaching you will ever do. The environment you create should be adult directed but child centered.

LOVE

Approach your children with love and caring, constantly strengthened by moments of excitement and joy. Tell your children how much you love them and care; distinguish for them that you may not *like* their behavior at a particular time but you always *love* them.

Touching has a remarkable impact on all children, providing an immediate sense of positive feedback and support while calming and giving a sense of security. It is a quiet, direct way of saying you care and can be used effectively to support behavior or to convey a sense of love while verbally redefining limits and acceptable behavior. It can convert discussions about negative behavior into those that leave positive memories.

Regardless of the kind of day it has been, always kiss your children goodnight and tell them how much you love them, even if you don't think they will understand. If your children are old enough, spend a few minutes reviewing both the good and bad parts of the day. Try not to let your children go to bed angry.

If it has been a bad day, it is phenomenally comforting and reassuring to go into your children's rooms after they are asleep and give them a little kiss. It is amazing how this single act puts everything into perspective, takes the sting out of a series of discipline and behavior problems, and lets you approach the next day with new enthusiasm, energy and vitality.

HIGH-QUALITY TIME

Fathers must focus on maximizing high-quality time. Meaningful, interactive activities support and promote your children emotionally, socially and intellectually. This should be a warm and accepting time. By providing this time for total focus, the impact of limited time availability is minimized and you as a parent can develop a very special, close and nurturing relationship with your children, while meeting the demands of work. It is essential that you separate work from this special time to allow you to focus on your children.

Design activities so there is balance between structured experiences and those that allow for creativity, inquisitiveness and self-direction. Provide time for talking, reflecting and for quiet. Allow for venting energy and frustration within the limits you have set for acceptable behavior. Experiences should be diverse, so your children can demonstrate their intellectual strength and also grow in leadership and athletic skills.

COMMUNICATION and LIMIT SETTING

Communication is crucial in any family unit and must be based on honesty and openness. Avoid surprises and explain new experiences in detail. Listen and talk to your children. Children need to be listened to; otherwise, they think they are being ignored and have nothing worthwhile to say. Attention-getting behavior may evolve quickly if your children think they are being ignored. Establish an environment in which your children recognize that you and other adults are listening and receptive to their words. Otherwise, it is difficult to expect children to listen.

Your children will identify their wishes, and it is crucial that you define age-appropriate limits in a consistent, definitive fashion. Consistency must be the basis for behavior modification. All adults caring for your child must impose comparable limits; without them, messages about what they can and cannot do remain unclear and the boundaries of acceptable behavior remain undefined. Children should be allowed to do most things, but there are certain things that are off-limits or unallowable. Touching the electric cord, eating the plant, throwing food, or screaming when things don't go their way are all common behaviors that are part of growing up; however, you need to control these behaviors. Setting firm limits is the only way to modify such behavior and discourage your children from repeating them.

Although your children will constantly test these limits, your guidelines will provide them with a sense of security, identity and structure. Any hesitancy or inconsistency on your part will be quickly recognized, and temper tantrums and uncontrollable behavior will be reinforced as a result. Without consistency, your relationship and expectations become unclear.

Positive responses and praise create an environment in which your children feel secure and comfortable. Provide constant feedback and reassurance to develop independence within appropriate boundaries. Touching provides immediate security and is reassuring for you and your children. Your response can assist to either add or subtract new behavioral patterns. Rarely does just one episode solidify and define a new limit or a behavioral pattern as acceptable or unacceptable; repetition of limit setting is essential since children will constantly test and retest these limits.

Pay attention to good behavior. If your child cleans up, doesn't throw the bottle or goes to bed quietly, provide positive reinforcement. Tell him or her how proud you are! If there are several problems, try to focus on the one "bad behavior" that bothers you the most; stopping this will hopefully reduce negative discussions and nagging. Remember that changes don't happen all at once but are the result of support and consistency. Emphasize that you love your child, you just don't like his or her behavior.

Avoid angry, negative words by keeping perspective and a sense of humor about your children's latest activities and antics. Maintain your cool and listen instead of getting mad. Repeated "No's" must be curtailed and, if possible, modified to positive answers. Divert your child's attention with activities that are not problematic.

You must allow your children to experiment and accept challenges while taking age-appropriate risks. Applaud your children for exercising new skills and abilities. Don't tease your children if they are timid about trying something; give praise when they do.

Certain activities, such as trips, visits to friends or restaurants, do need limits. Try to prepare your children so you can create a positive experience rather than one full of restrictions.

Don't convert what should be a fun activity into one that is filled with stress for everyone.

Within this framework, discipline is a mandatory part of raising children; it must be done consistently and without hesitation. Remain cool. Make a direct statement about what was done wrong and then follow through. Do not give repeated warnings or plead with your children. This merely demonstrates indecision and encourages whining.

The most effective means of disciplining children is to withdraw privileges, usually combined with a time-out or quiet time for a specific period in a well-defined place in the house. One of the least effective mechanisms of discipline is physical force; a spanking or a slap is quickly forgotten, transient and inappropriate. Physical force is rarely useful and often leads to an unhealthy relationship. If you feel your children need to be spanked, stop for a minute and think about alternatives before proceeding; spanking should only be used, if ever, for behaviors that are dangerous to your children or others.

Your children will quickly learn that negative behavior leads to specific losses. It is a mistake to let children call your bluff; don't be intimidated—be consistent, hard-nosed, and stand up to your children. Otherwise, the message conveyed is very confusing and your children will think they can "get away with it." Don't make it a "war of wills" between you and your child; both sides lose and get frustrated with these kinds of struggles. Children actually don't want everything they ask for but will constantly test the limits you place on them.

Equally important, children and their behavior must be put into perspective; remember that they should not be allowed to control the family and household. Until appropriate limits are established and behavior becomes acceptable, family functioning will be disrupted. Make sure your expectations and limits are reasonable, given your children's ages.

Your children learn from their environment and draw much of their self-image from it. Children are largely the product of a self-fulfilling prophecy. They become what people think of them. Children who are made to feel worthless and degraded will come to believe in their own worthlessness, while those who are held in high regard have much greater self-esteem. This should be remembered!

FAMILY NIGHT

As your children get older, initiating a family night can be useful in many families. It creates a sense of identity and guarantees communication and sharing. The dinner hour is an excellent time to savor and protect the family cohesiveness by establishing rules that provide few if any disruptions. These occasions should avoid judgmental approaches and focus on subjects that are of interest to the entire family. Everyone should have a chance to be heard in a positive and open manner. If the discussion lags, questions that may be asked include:

1. What was the best thing that happened today?
2. Tell me something good about the baby sitter, work, school, camp, etc.
3. In what way did you help someone or did someone help you today?
4. What did you do today that was a new experience?

PROBLEM SOLVING

Teach your children to solve problems. This allows them to deal with overwhelming situations and to convert them into positive experiences. Problem solving helps children to gain control over situations in a rational, logical fashion. Children can be taught by example to approach situations calmly and to identify problems, define options, evaluate possible outcomes and then choose the best solutions. This allows stress to be dealt with in a constructive fashion. If children are not taught to solve problems and to assume responsibility for defining solutions, the problems are no longer theirs. Leave appropriate problems where they correctly belong—on your children's shoulders.

PARENTAL BURNOUT

Parental burnout is an important factor to guard against in raising children. The time and energy commitments required to raise children can result in physical and emotional exhaustion. Time becomes a limited commodity. Those at greatest risk are parents who try to provide everything for their children, feeling guilt when they cannot meet their own expectations, either because their children cannot achieve some goal, there isn't enough money, or they don't have the flexibility to allow their children to participate in a given activity. Parents may begin to feel that they are not adequate and that their children are overly demanding. They sense that their family life is out of control. Children may not be appreciative of all the sacrifices that have been made. Although in extreme circumstances parental burnout may lead to child abuse, in most situations parents become dysfunctional and often retreat to isolation or turn to alcohol or drugs. Be aware if you feel that things are deteriorating. Find a way to unwind and decompress the situation rapidly.

Re-establish priorities and develop mechanisms that protect you when you feel overwhelmed; develop a support system. Figure out reasonable logistics for child care, car pooling etc., and reduce routine time required for chores at home.

Feeling good about yourself is important. Set realistic goals and expectations; communicate them and make sure you talk about frustrations. Protect your spouse by taking a trip, going out to dinner, exercising or enjoying some other activity that takes you away from your children periodically. Set aside specific time on a routine basis to re-establish a sense of intimacy with your wife that you may have lost with the many pressures of family and work. If you are a single parent, it is equally important to preserve "adult" time, to allow yourself to maintain relationships with close friends and family. Escape is sometimes necessary to regain perspective and composure.

FACILITATING DEVELOPMENT

Beyond your nurturing role, focus on your children's development of knowledge, skills and social comfort. Reading, activities, playing with toys and other interactions should be age-appropriate and provide a positive environment for learning and growth (see Ch. 6). Follow clues to your children's creativity, allowing them to explore and use their imagination in play and art. Children with handicaps or chronic disease have additional needs when setting up an optimal physical and emotional environment. Provide lots of materials for experimentation.

Remember that it is important to allow your children to take age-appropriate risks. Give them a chance to experiment with new skills and to overcome anxiety. Support them as they expand their horizons.

Raising your children must be based on love, quality time, and consistency from all caretakers; communication should be open and honest. Always convey love and caring. Above all, *enjoy your children and be proud of your relationship.* At the same time, recognize frustrations and keep them in perspective.

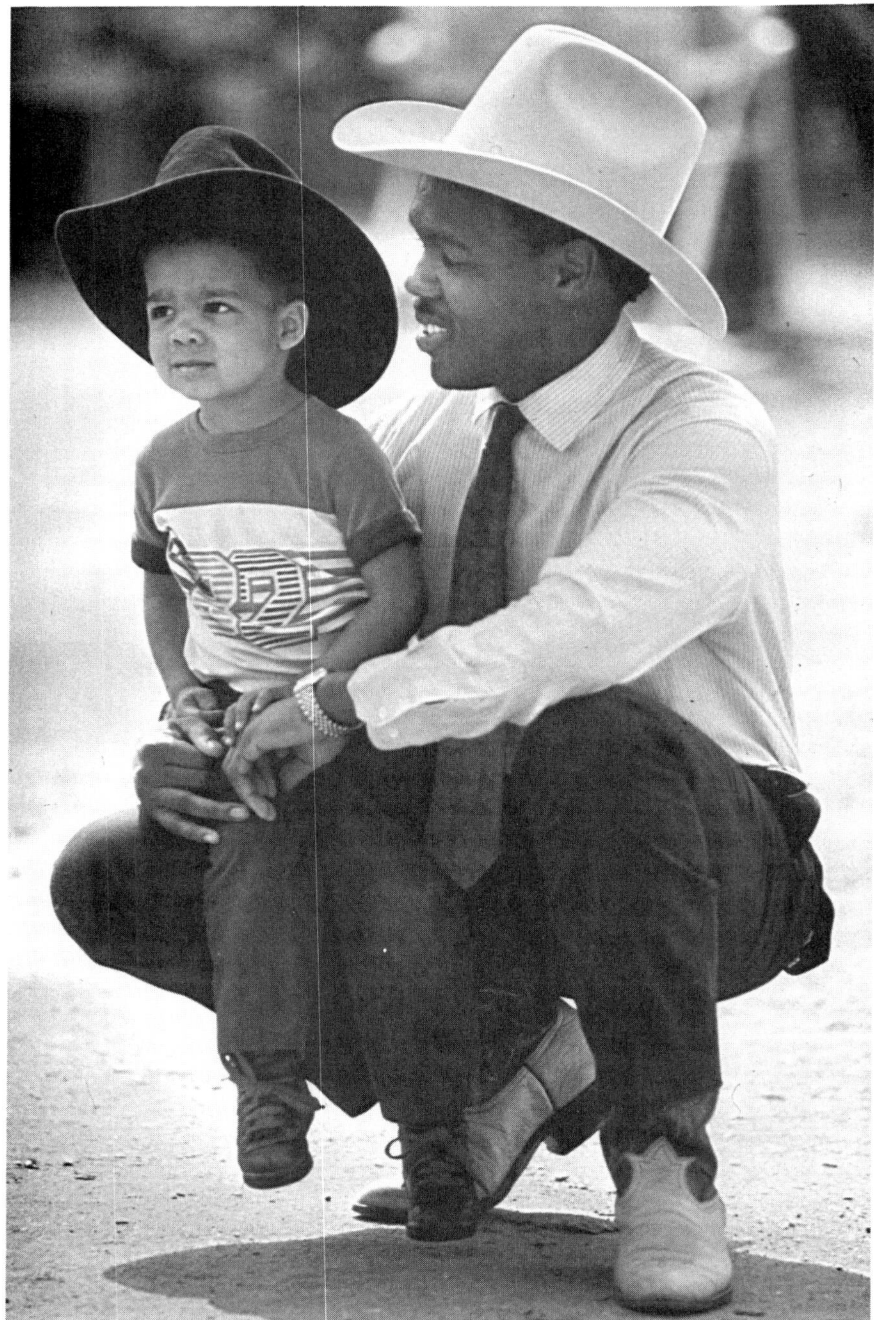

CONTEMPORARY ISSUES and CHALLENGES

Chapter 3

Changes in parenting have had a phenomenal impact on our children and on us. As dads and as parents, we must be increasingly aware of these evolving issues to help us understand some of the concerns, pressures and anxieties that we create for our children. In many respects there is more security in the family when both parents are actively involved in nurturing and child rearing. However, this brings new stresses.

Coupled with the enhanced mobility of our society and the dissolution of extended families, new issues have come to the forefront. These issues are discussed here to provide background and perspective, but clearly they require more exploration and definition before their impact can be measured.

MATERNAL EMPLOYMENT

The increasing number of women in the work force has produced changes in the paternal role. Forty-eight percent of U.S.

women with children under one year of age have jobs compared with only one-third of this group in 1975. Sixty-three percent of mothers with children four to five years old presently have jobs, up from 45 percent in 1975.

Increased maternal employment has resulted from numerous factors including a greater acceptance of women in the work force outside the household, diminished harassment and women's escalating interest in developing interests and a career independent of the family setting. The financial reality that two incomes are often required to maintain a desired standard of living has also played a dominant role. In some families where finances are not a paramount issue, the mother doesn't actually begin a new career or go back to work but gets increasingly involved with a community or civic organization as a key volunteer leading to significant commitments outside of the home.

A common question is whether there is an ideal time for mothers to begin or return to work. Parallel questions are now being asked by fathers. There is clearly no one answer; the decision must reflect the children's adjustment and development, financial and personal priorities, employment flexibility and maternal health. Parents may worry about missing important developmental stages of their infants, but the evidence suggests that this is not necessarily a problem if spending time with their children is a high priority.

Working parents can easily spend an average of four to six hours daily with their children during waking hours if this is a priority for nonworking time. This minimizes the impact of the work place.

As your wife begins planning to return to work, it is essential to find good child care that is stable, consistent, loving and caring (see suggestions later in this chapter). When you find a setting that you are comfortable with, returning to work becomes a more positive event. It is essential to be honest about any ambivalence related to returning to work. It is often useful for you and your wife to try to reduce the workload both at home and at work and be realistic in expectations.

The impact of maternal employment on children has been studied in great depth in many socioeconomic and cultural environments. The findings have not been uniform, but the trends have been consistent. While generalizations can be helpful, it is crucial to acknowledge that each child's needs must be considered separately and that any study results must be balanced by directly watching the impact on your child. Again, it is the quality not the quantity of time that leads to effective parenting.

Infants and young children do not suffer from a working mother if the day-care arrangements are high quality and involve significant ongoing interaction and stimulation. These additional attachments do not interfere with the primary relationship with parents. Children of working mothers may actually be better adjusted and demonstrate higher intellectual functioning. The mother-child relationship remains strong if it is constantly supported and strengthened and is a primary focus of family activity.

School-aged daughters of employed mothers tend to have consistently high academic performance. They tend to develop close relationships with their fathers if the fathers are warm, supportive and active participants in parenting. School-aged sons tend to have better social and personality adjustments as well as higher academic achievement when their mothers work. However, sons of lower socioeconomic families with a working mother may be less admiring of their dads, perhaps because of the perceived notion of economic failure on the part of their father. This may be an important observation to recognize during the early months of maternal employment.

Adolescents benefit when their moms work. Employed mothers (or mothers with significant interests or activities outside of the home) are usually happier, more satisfied and more likely to encourage their children to be independent. Sons tend to have better social and personal adjustment at school while daughters tend to be more outgoing, independent, motivated and adjusted to their environment. Children of working mothers are less likely to have stereotyped perceptions of life roles on the basis of being male or female.

PATERNITY LEAVE

The evolving role of fathers within the family and the concept of shared parenting have led some corporations to develop paternity-leave policies. These leaves can serve as an excellent introduction to fatherhood by allowing time to learn about and enjoy a new baby.

Paternity leave exists in a number of corporations, but fewer than 1 percent of eligible dads use them. Barriers to the use of paternity leave include the financial burden on the family from loss of income and the subtle work place pressure to define work as the highest priority. Many foreign industrialized countries provide routine paternity leaves to facilitate the involvement of the father in the care of their infants.

Legislation has been introduced in the United States to guarantee paternity leave for several weeks with provisions for reinstatement to the same job without loss of seniority and with protection from harassment. In the interim, informal solutions have evolved. One approach has been to work part time for a period or to adopt flexible working hours and a shorter work week. Flexibility of hours is tremendously useful. Some fathers use "personal days" provided by many companies as paid leave for taking time off when the baby is born, for baby-sitting, unexpected illnesses or other activities related to child care. Some fathers share or split positions. These approaches provide a mechanism to reduce conflict between home and work responsibilities but are clearly temporary measures. The ultimate balance must reflect the financial pressures and responsibilities of the work place and the home.

CHILD CARE

Some arrangement for child care is essential in families with employed parents and young children. The increasing number of mothers in the work force and the turmoil within the nuclear family are resulting in earlier exposure to group experiences that enhance children's educational, social and developmental skills. Services are now used by children of working and nonworking mothers.

If you or your wife decide to delay returning to work beyond four months, which is a common age for initiating child care, take your child's developmental stage into consideration. By 10 to 12 months of age, stranger anxiety is reduced and movement around the house increased, providing another good time to return to your previous activities. By 18 to 24 months, children are more social and comfortable with walking. Remember, your decision must necessarily be a balance between your child's adjustment and development, the desire to return to work or outside activities and financial pressures. It is an individual decision without any absolutes.

Diverse options are now available. Parent(s) or relatives can care for children as a primary responsibility, one of the parents can run a free-lance business in the home, parents can stagger their work hours or an older child may care for a younger one. An extension of this approach is to have someone come to your house to provide child care. This person must be carefully interviewed to assure that he/she is mature enough to provide loving and consistent care and deal with emergencies. The caregiver must understand the nature of the obligation and the expectations with respect to children and housekeeping chores. Make certain that your children like the person. Lastly, pay the person adequately. Advantages to having someone come to your house include the close personal relationship that develops between the caregiver and your child, convenience, familiarity with the setting, control of limits and expectations and the possibility of alleviating some housekeeping chores. Problems stemming from the relatively unskilled nature of such a baby sitter, if not well screened, include a lack of socialization for the child and the high cost associated with private child-care arrangements.

More commonly, child-care services develop within the community. Your children may go to another home where a few children are taken care of. These services are usually licensed within some kind of structure, may be cheaper and may have more flexible hours. They also provide a good opportunity for peer interaction.

Large professional centers can be either for profit or nonprofit. They have more highly trained staffs who are interested in early childhood education and development and may also have the resources to buy safe equipment and furniture. Although they all are licensed, the quality may vary. It is important that large groups be divided into units to allow a close relationship between children and caregivers.

Throughout this large group of child-care choices, there is little consistency of licensing and monitoring of the quality of service provided. The quality of child care is largely dependent on the caring, loving, interest and enthusiasm of the caregivers, so it is essential to evaluate the staff carefully. Issues concerning equipment, physical space, individual approaches to child care and preparations for illness must also be evaluated.

Planning for child care usually should begin during pregnancy or shortly thereafter to determine which options appear most feasible and to figure out what steps to take. Friends, newspapers, colleges and graduate schools can be useful referral sources. Develop a list of your needs and define whether you want a structured or nonstructured environment, a home or a large center. Consider details such as cost, hours, required flexibility, etc. Interview potential providers. Visit the child-care setting without your child, asking specific questions about licensing, hours and cost. Evaluate the background of the personnel, attitudes toward discipline and preparations for the children's safety and health. Observe the environment and the children's interactions. There should be an organized procedure for emergencies. Specific characteristics of caregivers may include:

1. Happy, warm and affectionate personalities. Use of encouragement, suggestion and praise rather than negative feedback;
2. Respect for the individual characteristics of children and, optimally, specific training in child care and development or many years of experience;
3. Shared values and consistency in discipline;
4. Staff works well together and children appear happy; understanding of development and changing behavior, and ability to stimulate children with art, music, etc.

After you have chosen the best alternative, introduce your child to the setting and the personnel if the child care is provided outside the home. If someone is coming to your home, have him/her visit with you and your child while you are there. As you begin to use child care, plan at first to spend extra time when you drop off your child or when the caregiver arrives.

Once you are comfortable with your decision, it is essential to spot-check by arriving home or at the facility unannounced. This provides an excellent opportunity to evaluate the use of time and the general attitude toward the children and observe firsthand the interactions between staff and children. Another safeguard is to be certain that your children are happy and positive about going to day care. Ultimately this is the best measure.

Beyond selecting an option, it is imperative to develop contingency plans if your child gets sick, your baby sitter becomes ill or some other problem develops that may require an immediate change in plans. Often this falls on the parent or close friend with the most flexibility in hours and responsibilities. Such arrangements may need to be different for sporadic one-day illnesses versus events that cause prolonged problems for either your child or caretaker.

It is essential that the caregiver always knows how to reach you during the day should some emergency arise. A caregiver must also know how to initiate cardiopulmonary resuscitation (Ch. 7) and how to rapidly call for emergency medical help in your absence (usually 911).

Some children spend an enormous amount of time in day care. If this is indeed quality time, it can work well as discussed in Ch. 2. Dependable child care is essential for everyone's mental and emotional health. When day care is good, it is a tremendous source of comfort; when things are not going smoothly, it is disruptive and emotionally draining.

Employment of both parents can be beneficial for everyone, but it requires excellent child-care arrangements and parents who provide a rich, warm and caring experience when they are home. Patience and persistence will eventually allow for this balance to work.

A somewhat related area of concern is finding baby sitters you feel comfortable with for several hours. It is imperative for you and your wife to get away periodically. Review a few steps before you leave:

1. Make sure important phone numbers are available, as outlined in Ch. 7;
2. Make sure you are comfortable with the baby sitter's maturity, relationship with your children and approach to discipline. Let your children get to know the baby sitter before you leave. Discuss specifics of feeding, bathing and sleeping;
3. Show the sitter around your house, pointing out specific escape routes, potential problems, unusual noises, etc.;

4. Make certain that your sitter knows where you will be, how to reach you and when you expect to be home. Calling at least once during the evening is reassuring.

"LATCHKEY" CHILDREN

In many two-career and single-parent families, older children who are able to care for themselves return home after school to a home with no adult present. This arrangement may not be ideal, but it is a realistic solution in many families. However, it is essential for parents and their children to discuss this at length to minimize the sense of isolation and loneliness that some children may feel.

Communication must be a specific emphasis for parents. If you must leave before your children go to school, telephone early and tell them good morning and how much you love them. After school, children need to tell someone about how good or bad their day was and to share their feelings. You can provide them with the opportunity by calling them when they arrive home and calling again later if you will be home late.

When you arrive home after work, spend time solely with your children, discussing the day and sharing the excitement of new adventures and triumphs.

Explain to your children why both you and your wife work. Express the positives by emphasizing that this gives mom and dad a chance to learn, contribute and spend time with colleagues during the day when children are usually in school. Working also allows the family to afford activities such as vacations.

Emphasize to your children the independence and trust you have placed in them. Some children enjoy having time to complete their homework and to relax without chores, while others prefer to earn additional allowance by doing chores.

Leave your children with a list of phone numbers, including their doctor, your office, neighbors, an ambulance service, and fire and police departments. Review other steps to be taken in case of emergency. You should also emphasize that if your children are feeling lonely or just want to talk, that you can be reached by phone. Be available for them when they call. Make sure they don't let strangers know that they are home alone. Some communities have set up special hot lines for such children.

ABDUCTION

Children disappear each year from their neighborhoods, houses, yards and schools. Many children run away themselves, responding to the stress and pressures of home. Others are taken by strangers or abducted by a separated parent who does not have custody. Many of these children are harmed.

Teach your children how to prevent such occurrences. You should periodically review a number of common-sense rules with your children, prefacing the topic with a discussion of how much you love them and how you never want anything bad to happen. These rules include:

1. Do not talk to strangers. Never accept gifts or rides;
2. Do not help strangers who ask you to get into their car in order to show directions;
3. Never answer the door for strangers;
4. If alone at home, don't let strangers know;
5. Do not allow anyone to play with your genital ("private") region;
6. Do not keep secrets from parents, even if you are afraid to tell them because someone told you to keep it quiet;
7. If you get lost in a store, find a clerk and ask for help. Do not walk out of the store;
8. Do not go places without adult supervision.

Other guidelines to be aware of include:

1. Parents should be careful not to leave children unsupervised in the car, grocery cart or front yard;
2. Parents should teach children how to use the phone and make certain they know their phone number and address and have some idea of how to get home;
3. Parents should discuss reliable sources of help wherever children may be, including police officers, mail carriers, store clerks, etc.;
4. Parents should not put their children's names on clothing since abductors may use the names as an introduction. Instead, use some distinctive mark that children can easily identify;
5. Parents should be certain day-care settings and schools have specific rules on who can pick up their children.

DISCUSSING where BABIES COME FROM

As your children get older, questions about babies will come up, particularly if another child is expected. Much of the discussion must reflect your own value system, but several steps may be useful in the educational process. During much of the toddler years, you will develop games that focus on naming body parts; the genitalia must be incorporated into these games. Do not make the distinction between boys and girls based upon negatives. Emphasize that boys have a penis and that girls have a vulva, vagina and clitoris.

Although this is often an awkward subject, the best way to handle questions about where babies come from is to be straightforward and comfortable with your answers. Use words and descriptions that your child can understand and make certain that the process you describe implies *active* participation by both you and mom; it is a joyful process based upon mutual respect, love and wishes.

Children will ask how babies are made. One good response is to say, "Mommies and daddies make babies. Mommy carries the baby while it is growing. When the baby is ready to be born, Mommy and Daddy go to the hospital and help your new brother (sister) come out."

During this process, it is essential to communicate your personal value system regarding sexual mores. It is often worth emphasizing to your children that they shouldn't play with other children's genitalia. Masturbation and self-exploration are natural; it is important to allow some of this to occur as part of normal behavior.

DIVORCE and the SINGLE DAD

Separation and divorce are difficult for children as well as for adults. Communication is essential; both parents should sit down and discuss the separation or divorce with their children. Unless specifically addressed, children may feel that if they had been "better," their parents would still be happy together. Parents should clearly explain that the problem is between mom and dad and not because of anything the children did. Children can often understand that their parents still love one another but have trouble living together. Divorce is hardest on toddlers and early elementary school children whose personalities are forming and whose dependency needs are great. The transitions and changes occurring during divorce are smoother if anger, disruption and unhappiness are minimized and worked out between parents in private rather than in front of children.

Be very specific in describing what your children's lives will be like and when they will see their parents. Emphasize the things that will be the same such as meals, stories, visiting grandparents, etc. This must be discussed in age-appropriate terminology. Be concrete, positive and upbeat; convey the love that you have and the security and stability you are building into the new relationship.

Custody arrangements vary following divorce. One parent may become the primary caregiver; increasingly, joint custody is established with equal time commitments from the parents. Sixty-eight percent of children live with both biological parents, 20 percent live in single-parent households, 9 percent live with a biological parent and a stepparent, and 4 percent live with neither parent. More than half of children of divorced parents see their absent parent less than once a month.

Parents must share in the decision making and be consistent in demands and expectations. It requires communication and cooperation for this to work. Identify your children's needs and make sure they are met. Provide a reliable structure with enough flexibility to respond to changing needs and expectations, special occasions and growth.

If you or your former wife are concerned about one of your children, sit down and talk about the changes that are occurring. Make certain that your priorities are clear, your expectations defined and your approaches consistent. Without such periodic discussions, problems are inevitable and children will be insecure and unsure of their relationships and positions in your respective families.

Single parenting presents unique challenges to fathers because the importance of developing a trusting and secure relationship is crucial to the healthy growth of children. Single parents must define priorities even more clearly and be certain that the balance between work, personal needs and family is comfortable. Develop back-up resources including friends, work associates and family to share some of the responsibilities and to reduce isolation for both the single parent and his children. Activities for both you and your children can often be shared with other single parents and extended families.

Specific suggestions for the single father may be helpful in trying to create a framework for your children and a positive attitude toward women:

1. Be available and listen; provide warmth and sensitivity;
2. Provide mother surrogates if mom is unavailable: Girl Scouts, play groups, Big Sisters, etc.;
3. Develop responsibility, positive self-image and independence within your children;
4. Focus on the future and the positives of relationships;
5. Maintain a relationship with your extended family.

Should you become a single parent as a result of the death of your spouse, the depth of the loss will be jointly shared by you and your children. Support from family, friends and others is essential as you begin to grieve and feel the tremendous loss and emptiness that exist while you try to put your own life back together, support your children and begin to create a new meaning for "family." Putting the pieces back together is often long and painful; draw upon whatever resources you can mobilize. Often such a loss tightens the family unit, and you may find strength, love and warmth from your children as you provide similar support to them.

TALKING about DEATH

Children may need to deal with the death of a friend, relative or peer. This must be handled with sensitivity and compassion to be certain that the understanding is correct and the response appropriate.

The response to death is largely a reflection of previous death-related experiences and the child's pattern of responding to emotional turmoil. It is hard to explain death to children; occasions such as the death of a fish or a pet can serve as introductions to the topic. This may help prepare them to understand, but explanations are taken very literally. Children may have sleep problems if death is described as "sleeping forever" or similar euphemisms. Children may ask the same question again and again, trying to reach some understanding of what "death" means. Always be honest and do not say things like "he has gone away." Convey the sense of separation and permanency, but make certain they understand that they did not contribute to the death.

It is important not to exclude your children from the mourning and grieving process. Children often wish to go to the funeral of a friend or relative, but this must be weighed against the stresses on parents. For many, the funeral provides a focus for the mourning and grieving process and children should be allowed to share in this process. Children want to know about, but may have trouble understanding, the reality of death. Because their fantasies are usually worse than the reality, many benefit from being a part of this process. If you decide not to have your children attend the funeral, you may want to take them to the funeral home beforehand, discuss the funeral with them or go to the cemetery later. Children do learn to understand the finality of death. During grieving and mourning they can help adults keep perspective on the meaning and value of life. Often your physician, community religious leade, or a close friend can be helpful in sorting out these issues.

Deaths of friends or grandparents raise many issues for children. A common one is the question, "What would happen if my parents died? Who would take care of me?" To make certain this does not create emotional anguish, reassure your child.

If a parent has died, the sense of loss and grief is immeasurable, particularly given the tremendous pain and sorrow that the surviving spouse is feeling. Friends, family, community leaders and work associates can all play an important role in supporting the children as well as the adults. Outside help is essential! As the immediate event becomes more distant, a restructuring of the family can help recreate the relationship between the surviving parent and the children.

Children deal with death in much the same way as adults, although the grief process is often not permitted to run its full course. Children can mourn and grieve and should be allowed to do so. Regression in established behaviors is common, as are intermittent guilt and anger. Often children express their inner feelings through play; this should be watched and used to better understand your children's reactions. The time following a death is difficult for the entire family. Be sensitive to this and make certain that activities and stability slowly return to normal.

It is important to provide young children with positive memories. It is often useful to sit down with a photo album that recaptures good memories of the deceased and talk about what was happening. This concrete approach can be reassuring to your children and can serve as a means of opening up communication. It may also be helpful for the entire family to focus on the numerous events that allow us to remember people fondly.

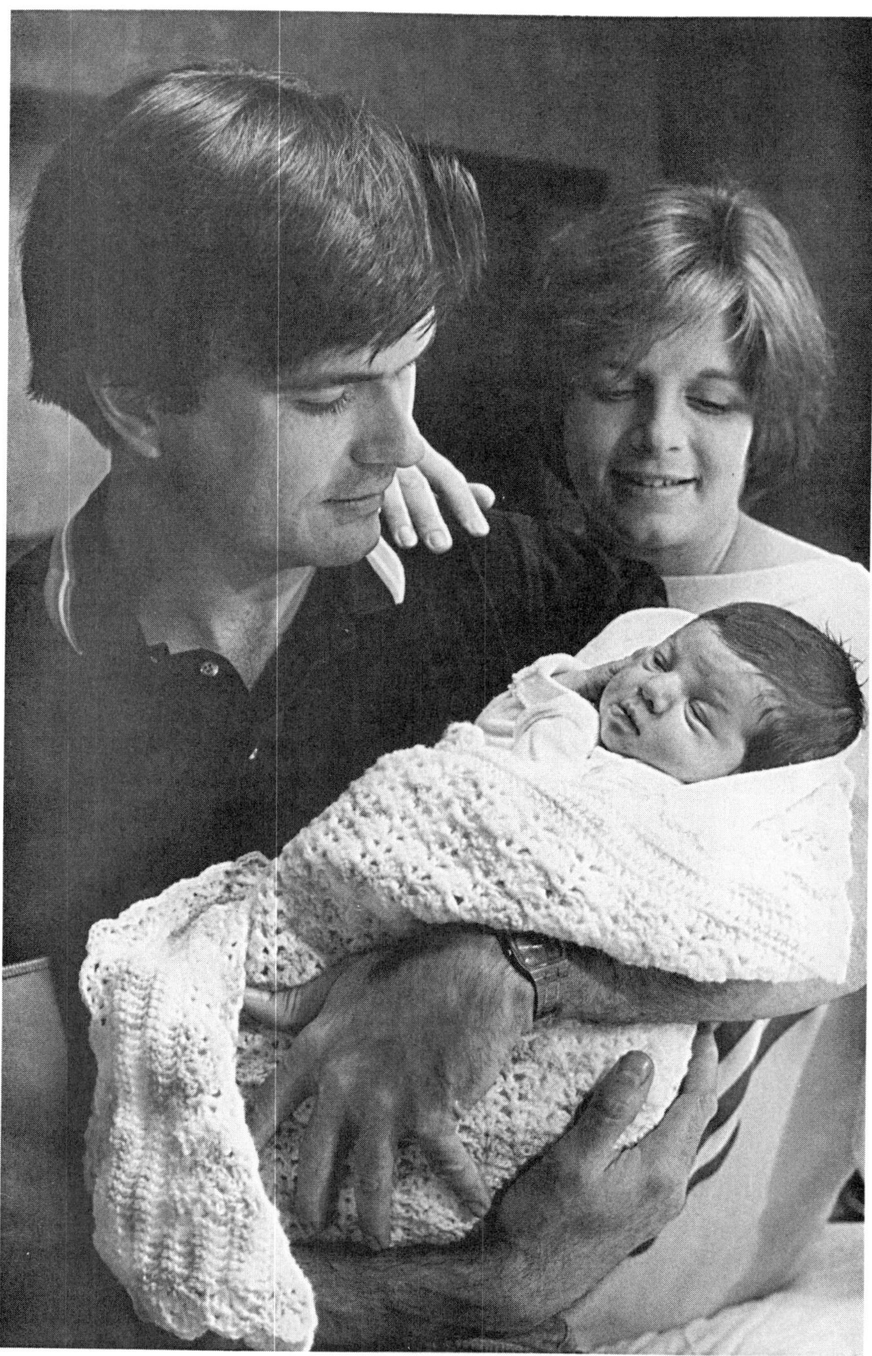

YOUR NEW BABY the NUTS and BOLTS

✦

Chapter 4

✦

Having a baby is a family affair. Couples become pregnant, not just moms and, indeed, you will both enjoy and share in pregnancy. Immense physical changes occur during the three trimesters, reflecting the rapid growth of the fetus, hormonal changes, the growing anticipation and the excitement of the impending addition to the family. You may often have symptoms similar to your wife's. You may have the nausea of the first trimester or the fatigue of the third. Some dads even gain weight and develop specific dietary cravings. Your excitement will grow as the weeks unfold. It is not unusual to be anxious about your wife and new baby's health, your willingness to share your wife's affections and time, your fathering capabilities and your ability to support your expanded family.

In fact, sharing the anxiety associated with the pregnancy and your baby's health is important. Fathers can be tremendously helpful in supporting mom through the emotional variability of the first trimester and the discomfort and concerns of the third. Extra support and understanding are mandatory. Chores and activities that were once done without a second thought now become tiresome and burdensome. Relax and set priorities for routine activities to reduce day-to-day demands. Talk about concerns, anxieties and problems. Your initial anxieties will be quickly replaced by competency and enjoyment as you all share in the wonder of your baby.

PREPARING for YOUR NEW BABY

Participate in childbirth-preparation classes such as those that teach Lamaze techniques. Classes about children and childbirth can help you understand what to expect and encourage your involvement and commitment. Read and talk to others about pregnancy and delivery. Choose the place of birth carefully; hospitals, birthing rooms and centers, and home birth have broadened the options but should be discussed with your family practitioner or pediatrician and obstetrician. Often, a visit and tour of the hospital or birthing center is helpful. (Note: The term "hospital" will be used to simplify the discussion: the preparation required applies to all settings.)

Prepare for your trip to the hospital: know the route, arrangements for parking, and the registration process (preregistration when offered is advisable). Make arrangements for your wife to get to the hospital in case you are at work or out of town. During the anticipation period, complete your baby's room, start a baby book, put the car seat in the car, keep your car in good mechanical condition and filled with gas, make arrangements for someone to care for your other children, and have your wife's doctor's phone number as well as a list of people you want to call once your baby has arrived.

As the delivery approaches, make sure your wife always knows where you are. Pack an overnight bag for you and your

IMPORTANT PHONE NUMBERS

Wife's doctor's name ______________ Phone __________

Hospital ______________ Phone __________

Address ______________

Labor and delivery phone ______________

Emergency department phone ______________

Nursery phone ______________

Ambulance ______________ Phone __________

Taxi ______________ Phone __________

Neighbor or friend (for help)

Name ______________ Phone __________

Name ______________ Phone __________

Baby sitter ______________ Phone __________

Address ______________

Family and Friends

Name ______________ Phone __________

Name ______________ Phone __________

Name ______________ Phone __________

Name ______________ Phone __________

Name ______________ Phone __________

Name ______________ Phone __________

Name ______________ Phone __________

Phone charge no. ______________

Special things to remember ______________

____

____

wife including a watch with a second hand. You may want a camera or video recorder; load the film before the big day. I will always remember having our first 24 pictures come out blank, having forgotten to load the camera correctly.

During a routine visit to your wife's doctor, you may want to discuss steps to take if you believe your baby's delivery is imminent and you are unable to reach the selected hospital. Are there closer hospitals that may be accessible? Should you call an ambulance, police, fire department? What should you do? Remember, it is always better to get to the hospital too early than too late!

You may also want to select your favorite girl's and boy's names based on personal preferences and such considerations as sound, meaning, rhythm with the middle and last names, familial factors and social implications. The choice of name is important and is a very personal decision based on the balancing of alternatives. The middle name is often excellent to acknowledge particular family members. Suggestions that should be considered in addition to those noted above include:

1. Choose serious names that your child will not outgrow;
2. Choose names that clearly identify your child's sex;
3. Usually avoid atypical names or unusual spellings;
4. Avoid trendy names.

If your wife visits an obstetrician, choose a pediatrician before delivery if possible. Family physicians commonly perform the delivery and follow your new baby's progress. Have a prenatal interview to be certain you are comfortable with your choice. A good match is important. Decide what questions you want to ask before your visit. Consider your doctor's training, competency, communication skills, approach to child rearing and policy for late-night and weekend emergencies. Determine the office location and hours, fees, availability, policy regarding phone calls and hospital affiliations. Talking with other parents may be useful.

In addition to the furniture and other items described in Ch. 5, make sure you have enough clothing and care items:

Diapers: If you decide to use cloth diapers, purchase four dozen diapers, a dozen diaper pins and vinyl protective pants (initially snap-on and then pull-on) and call a diaper service for rates. If you decide to use disposable diapers, you will need about

350 for the first month.

Clothing: Six undershirts with side snaps, socks or booties; three to six newborn gowns appropriate for the season; sweater and coat during cold weather.

Care items: Sheets (flannel-coated), fitted mattress cover, blankets, towels and washcloths; hairbrush, nail scissors, absorbent bibs (cloth diapers work well), receiving blankets and lap pads.

The support you and your wife can give to each other in the delivery room is emotionally exciting, and makes the delivery smoother while strengthening bonding. These moments are unique and unforgettable, solidify the experience of childbirth and mark the beginning of an entirely new phase in your life. You will remember them forever!

During labor and delivery you will be the confidant, supporter, coach and messenger. The contractions your wife feels represent the attempt to push your new infant out of the uterus. These contractions become more frequent and there may be some bloody discharge. The membranes may rupture with a release of water. Time the contractions and call your doctor when contractions reach the frequency he/she indicated (usually every two to four minutes), or if bloody discharge appears.

From here on it is a team effort among you, your wife, the nursing staff and your physician. Encourage and support your wife and focus your total attention on her. Help with the breathing and pushing. As the delivery becomes imminent, the excitement peaks and your team effort escalates. Finally the moment arrives and there is anticipation, excitement and obvious nervousness.

Once your doctors are sure that your baby is healthy, hold your baby and look and wonder about this miracle. In the nursery, all children are given a shot of vitamin K and have ointment placed in their eyes. A blood test before leaving the hospital and again two weeks later screens for a variety of congenital problems including PKU (phenylketonuria).

Even healthy children will often have temporary problems with low sugar or be somewhat yellow (jaundiced), the latter usually improving without special treatment.

On the first or second night, it is often nice to spend a little time alone with your wife and have a special, quiet moment such as a fancy dinner or an elegant dessert. Flowers or perfume are a nice additional touch. Then go home and get a good night's sleep. Remember your other children and get them actively involved right after the delivery (see Ch. 6 on sibling rivalry).

Get to know one another as members of a bigger family during your time in the hospital and afterward. Paternity leave, even if short, is essential for you to enjoy your new infant and to relax and experience the magic of growth and development. Use the time to get comfortable with feeding, bathing, diapering and just holding your baby. It should be a family time. If you have older children, make sure you involve them with the new baby and that they feel that they are having adequate contact and involvement with mom, dad and the new baby.

It is not uncommon for mothers to become depressed, tearful and emotionally distraught by the fifth day after delivery. Support and understanding are required.

Restrict visitors and don't get carried away with a sense that you need to entertain and worry about friends and family; there will be plenty of time for that later. Make certain that you and your wife have discussed these issues before delivery. You have to consider whether you will want your extended family to help and to what extent. Although in select circumstances this assistance is useful, in general this time should be reserved for you, your wife and your children to get to know one another. Don't complicate responsibilities and activities unnecessarily.

Although this book is not meant as a comprehensive manual of baby care, several common questions arise for dads and will be discussed briefly. Other chapters discuss development (Ch. 4 and Ch. 6), behavior (Ch. 6), and safety (Ch. 5) in detail.

FEEDING

Babies like to suck and eat. Choosing bottle or breast-feeding is a personal decision based on personal beliefs and logistical constraints. Mothers who elect to breast-feed often need reassurance until breast-feeding is firmly established over the first three to four days. Fathers can be very supportive of this. Be certain that mom has a good fluid intake and is feeling well. Of course, try to spare her from doing household chores. Early on, the breast may actually get too engorged, and you might suggest a breast pump (looks like a bicycle horn) or manual expression of milk to make it easier for your baby to grab onto the nipple. In general, babies are excellent gauges of how much they need to eat; let them provide you with the limits. The breasts work on a clear supply-and-demand principle; the more your baby demands, the more milk will be produced.

Supplements to breast-feeding—with the exception of occasional vitamins—should not be needed. In the first few days while flow is being established, supplements can interfere with the supply-and-demand relationship that the baby and breast are developing. If mom is on medicines or is ill, this may not be true. Later on, once breast-feeding is well established, bottles may be used sporadically or breast milk can be expressed and saved. This is an excellent chance for dad to participate in the feeding routine. If the 2:00 a.m.-feeding is a bottle, fathers often find that giving it is a terrific experience and helps mom get needed rest.

Bottle feeding is an excellent alternative. The formula you select should be discussed with your physician; most babies require no special formula. Formula comes ready-made, concentrated (add water before giving) or powdered (very easy to use and economical). Make sure that you read the directions carefully; mistakes can cause significant problems. Be careful to test the temperature of heated formula before serving. Personal preference and cost should determine your choice. Many people find that using powdered formula (one scoop for every two ounces of water) is particularly easy and economical since you can add warm water to a premeasured amount of powder in the bottle and not have to deal with warming. Formula contains vitamins so no supplement is needed. Discuss with your doctor whether you should use iron-supplemented formula; usually it is not required. Unmodified cow's milk is not appropriate for younger infants because it has more protein and sodium than recommended. Bottles must be carefully washed but generally, do not need to be sterilized. Do not bottle prop or put your baby to sleep with a bottle since this ultimately increases your child's chance of developing dental decay and ear infections.

Your baby may need five or six feedings a day and one or two during the night for the first few weeks; this frequency will decrease as your baby gets older. By one month of age, the interval between feedings can be stretched to every three to four hours. If permitted, your child could eat (or at least suck) every hour or two, but this will quickly lead to parental exhaustion. While feeding, try to pat your baby every three to five minutes and allow your infant to burp. Your child may tend to spit. This is relatively unimportant if your baby is growing well. Babies will usually outgrow it. If it is excessive, discuss the problem with your doctor. If your baby is spitting up a great deal, you might try to keep your baby upright for 30 to 45 minutes after feeding, burp more frequently, feed in smaller amounts or, lastly, thicken the food , after discussing it with your doctor. (See chalasia, page 209)

Solids do not have to be started until four to six months. Begin slowly with small-sized servings and remember that they are extra and should not replace milk. However, it is a fun activity to try solids and watch your child's messy response. Rice cereal for babies (mixed with breast milk or formula) is usually begun first, followed by vegetables, fruit and meat. You can also introduce barley and wheat cereals. The exact order can be varied depending upon personal preferences. Foods that should be avoided initially include tomatos, egg whites and chocolate. Raisins and peanuts should be avoided because of the risk of choking (Ch. 7). Both home-prepared and ready-made foods are fine.

Feeding issues for the older child are discussed in Ch. 6.

INFANT CARE

Baths

Bathe your infant with a sponge or washcloth and water during the first few weeks. You can do this on a table or lap or in a sink or special bath. Cleanse the base—where the umbilical cord was cut—with a clean cotton ball or swab soaked in alcohol.

After several weeks (especially after the naval and circumcision are healed), use a plastic bathtub or a sink with a small amount of water and very mild soap like Neutrogena or Dove. Avoid scalding water by adjusting the water heater down to 120° Fahrenheit; make sure the room is warm. Be careful to keep soap out of your baby's eyes. Rinse carefully. Rarely do you need any cream or ointment, but if your child has dry skin, a mild nonperfumed cream such as Nivea may be useful and certainly does no harm.

Diapers

Disposable or cloth diapers are fine. Disposables hug the legs to avoid leaking. Self-adhering tapes are usually attached. Many people prefer washable cloth diapers. To use them, place the diaper diagonally on the changing mat, fold it over forming a triangle, then place the baby on the diaper with the base of the triangle at the waist level. Bring the edges together and fasten with special, guarded safety pins. Some cloth diapers attach with Velcro. Plastic pants (available with Velcro if desired) are usually worn with cloth diapers. A diaper service helps make cloth diapers practical for busy families.

Clothing

Most clothes are sized by age and will quickly become too small. It is useful to buy them somewhat large to prolong their use. Choose easy-care colors, fabrics and styles that are fire retardant. When washing clothes, make sure they are double-rinsed. Consider adding a fabric softener. Don't spend money on shoes. Socks or booties are fine.

Many infants and newborns may continue to burp for weeks, so a burp towel (often a cloth diaper) is important to take along on all activities, whether for playing, feeding or just holding.

Pacifiers

Routine feeding satisfies some children while others benefit from pacifiers, which can help satisfy your child's desire to suck. Use commercial pacifiers that meet safety standards, are one piece and designed to prevent aspiration. Wash new pacifiers thoroughly before using and inspect them frequently. They do wear out; replace them if sticky, enlarged or cracked. Never put a pacifier on a string, since your baby could strangle.

Teething

Your child gets the first of 20 baby teeth at around six months of age. The two central lower teeth erupt first, followed by the upper pair. Minimal fever and diarrhea may accompany teething.

Cradle cap

Scaly skin on the scalp is common and usually responds to soft scrubbing of the head. Supplement once a week by shampooing with Selsun Blue or Sebulex. Do not use petroleum jelly products (Vaseline).

Fingernails

Periodically cut fingernails and toenails using special baby nail scissors that have no sharp edges.

Circumcision

Little boys who are not circumcised should have their foreskin gently pulled back without force and the underlying area cleansed with water. This is best done during baths. Those who have been circumcised will often have some redness and swelling around the penis for a few days. The decision to circumcise your son should be based on personal preference, religious, cultural and social factors, as well as whether you are circumcised.

Genitalia

Girls may have some swelling of the labia. During the first week of life, slight mucous or blood from the vagina may also be noted. This is normal. Both boys and girls may have some transient breast enlargement.

Safety

Safety is an important consideration. All equipment must be specially designed to avoid accidents as outlined in Ch. 5. Buy flame-retardant clothing, carefully protect heaters and electrical wiring, and keep your child away from hot liquids, foods and fireplaces. Avoid toys and other objects with sharp edges and those small enough to be inhaled or swallowed. Discard plastic bags and long cords. Always use a car seat.

DEVELOPMENT

Your child's rapid growth and development are perhaps the most exciting aspects of the first days after delivery. After a small decrease in weight during the first week, children gain an average of one ounce per day for the next month. Little muscle control is present, so the head must be supported. Talk to and entertain your child: infants have amazingly subtle responses to you in the early weeks. As new skills are gained, new responses appear.

The early weeks are for bonding, reflecting and enjoying. New things become evident on a daily basis, new noises are heard and new muscle control is acquired. Interactive play becomes increasingly essential, and your child will slowly learn to follow you and brightly colored objects in a very social manner (see Ch. 6).

Encourage your child's development. During the first few months, touching calms infants, while bright pictures, mirrors and hanging mobiles stimulate. Sing, talk rhythmically, laugh and interact with your child.

Later on, your baby will be able to look at the world from a sitting position. At this point, you will be able to interact more with your child by playing with balls, exploring different shapes and textures, dangling bright objects and playing with mirrors. At one year of age, your baby will enjoy looking at pictures and will begin to correlate them with words. Walking will become an essential part of exploration, and slowly your child will be able to draw shapes and designs with crayons.

ROUTINE VISITS and IMMUNIZATIONS

It is important to establish a comfortable relationship with a pediatrician or family practitioner. Your doctor should provide you with ongoing parenting and child-care information and make sure your new baby is growing, developing well and is fully protected from a variety of infections.

At each visit, your health-care provider will weigh and measure your child, check development, ask about special issues and concerns and perform a physical examination. Immunizations are administered according to a specific schedule.

Normal growth is essential. Your child's growth will be plotted to determine the pattern of growth and to make sure that everything is going well. You may want to follow your child's growth yourself on the charts provided at the end of this book (Appendix A). Remember that not all children are average; some must be bigger and some must be smaller. What is important is that your child follows his/her own growth curve.

Your health-care provider will also assess development. Many offices use screening tests, which can be reassuring that your child is following a normal pattern of development.

Routine visits will ensure normal growth and development assessment. Your doctor will check your child periodically, answer questions and provide routine screening. Go to these examinations as a family when possible; it's terrific fun.

The first *two-week visit* will allow your doctor to make certain that you and your wife are adapting well and that your infant is growing. Normally, by two weeks of age your baby will be at birth weight, having slightly fallen off in weight during the first week. A second PKU blood test will be done. This is an excellent time for you to ask questions about feeding, bowel movements, urination, sleep, sibling rivalry and safety precautions. You should discuss frustrations and fatigue.

At *two, four and six months*, your baby will be weighed again and checked. Your health-care provider should pay particular attention to the adjustment of the family, problems, conflicts, accident prevention and your baby's development. Your baby will receive diphtheria-tetanus-pertussis (whooping cough) and polio vaccines. Your baby's weight should double by five months of age.

No immunizations are given at *nine months*. This visit focuses on development and accident prevention. A Denver Developmental Screening Test (DDST) will often be given to check development and should serve as a take-off point for discussing your child's present status as well as what to expect in the next few months. Discuss any concerns.

At the *one-year visit*, your doctor will again review accident prevention and assess growth and development. Your infant's weight should have approximately tripled from that at birth.

The next immunization should be scheduled at between 15 and 18 months of age. Measles-mumps-rubella (MMR) vaccine as well as DTP and polio vaccine are recommended. A new Haemophilus influenzae (HIB) vaccine may be given at 18 months. Your health-care provider will give particular attention to accident and poison prevention, as well as behavior, weaning, discipline, toilet training and any frustrations that have surfaced.

At *two years*, your baby has phenomenal mobility in terms of walking and running and talks up a storm. "No" is an important part of the vocabulary (see Ch. 6).

From *three to five years*, your toddler will be seen annually to be certain that growth and development are normal, discipline and behavior are evolving nicely, and questions are answered. As always, safety issues need particular attention including street, bicycle and water safety. At five years, additional immunizations will be administered. During this period, routine health care should include a visit to a dentist to monitor the development and eruption of new teeth.

Recommended Immunization Schedule	
Two months:	DTP, polio
Four months:	DTP, polio
Six months:	DTP
15 to 18 months:	DTP, polio, measles, mumps, rubella (MMR); H. influenzae (HIB)
Four to five years:	DTP, polio

Discuss immunizations with your doctor so that you understand the risks and the benefits as well as the reactions you should look for following the shot.

Diphtheria-tetanus-pertussis (DTP) vaccine protects against diphtheria, which infects the throat and upper airway; tetanus (lockjaw), which causes muscle spasms; and pertussis (whooping cough), which results in severe coughing. All are potentially dangerous diseases. The vaccine does have certain immediate side effects or reactions (fever, irritability) and can have long-term problems (seizures, retardation), which should be discussed with your doctor. A great deal of controversy has developed related to this vaccine.

Polio vaccine given as drops protects against paralysis and has rare complications.

Measles-mumps-rubella (MMR) vaccine is a triple vaccine providing excellent protection with very few reactions.

Haemophilus influenzae type B (HIB) vaccine partially protects children from the leading cause of meningitis in early childhood.

Enjoy your new baby! Despite the responsibilities, frustrations and challenges, the fathering experience is one of the most exciting and rewarding you will ever have the pleasure of sharing.

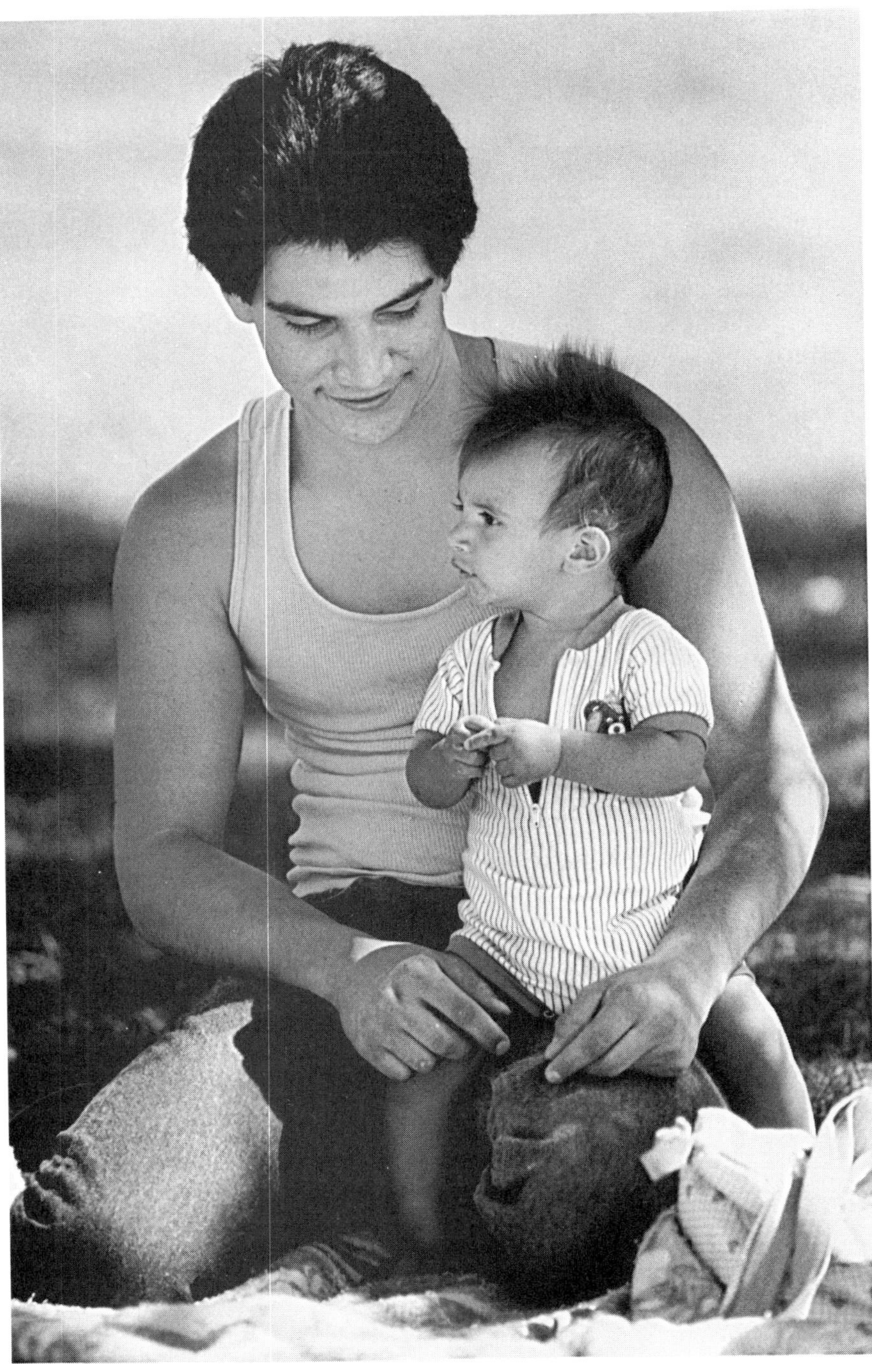

"BABY-PROOFING" your HOME

Chapter 5

Accidents represent a tremendous source of injury to your children, and are largely preventable with appropriate care and precautions. It is imperative that you keep your home safe on an ongoing basis to minimize the risks. As a father, you must realize that there will be accidents. You will probably feel guilty and distraught when they occur. Eliminating safety problems in your home goes a long way toward reducing such events. Furthermore, knowing how to respond may reduce short-term anxiety and long-term problems, as outlined in Ch. 8 on poisoning and Ch. 9 on injury. Exploration is essential; although this places your children in some danger, it is a necessary part of growth and a child's definition of normal independence.

ACCIDENT PREVENTION

Prevention is the key to avoiding injuries. Consider your children's ages and levels of development in determining what factors are risky and how to best reduce problems. Focus on taking these steps to "baby-proof" your home:

1. Keep sharp or dangerous objects out of reach of children. Choose furniture and equipment carefully;
2. Put safety latches on all drawers containing knives or potentially dangerous objects. Optimally, move dangerous objects to inaccessible areas;
3. Use protectors for electrical plug outlets. Tape down electrical cords to keep children from biting or pulling them;
4. Use special doorknobs and gates as needed;
5. Use safety straps or restraints when appropriate;
6. Always use car seats or seat belts;
7. Avoid areas where children could fall or where objects could tip over. Remove obstacles, check stairs and install handrails;
8. Avoid dangerous toys, plastic bags and cords longer than 12 inches that are attached to toys, drapes or other objects. Select toys so they are too large to cause choking, will not break or splinter, have safe paint, rounded edges and no long strings;
9. Avoid temperature extremes. Make certain that the hot water heater is turned down to 120° Fahrenheit or below;
10. Avoid small objects that may cause choking. This includes pacifiers that may break or have pieces;
11. Avoid drinking hot drinks and smoking while holding your baby;
12. Unplug potentially dangerous small electrical appliances;
13. Do not have firearms in the house;
14. Teach street, bicycle and water safety;
15. Store matches, gasoline and combustible liquids in a safe place. Screen fireplaces;
16. Teach everyone who cares for your child about safety.

Newborns

Safety for your new baby involves being careful and sensible, and purchasing appropriate and safe equipment. Using common sense is usually an adequate precaution once you have surrounded your child with safe toys, furniture and equipment. Be watchful! Specific criteria outlined at the end of this chapter should be helpful in deciding what to buy and how to further protect your child.

Infants

Use a car seat *all* the time. It is essential that you buckle up your child and yourself every time you get into the car. Not using a car seat that you have bought, or using it incorrectly, is of *no* value. Make certain that all equipment and furniture in your house are appropriate for your child's developmental stage.

Safety-proof your house by eliminating potentially dangerous products and objects from the grasp of your adventuresome, crawling, climbing, resourceful child. Look at where you store items. Get down to your child's level; this provides a useful perspective in defining potential dangers. You will be amazed by what you will find.

Environmental dangers also exist. Take the following precautions:

1. Limit sun exposure to avoid burns;
2. Restrict access to water and never leave your children alone during a bath;
3. Do not allow your children to chew on electrical wires or potentially dangerous plants;
4. Prevent burns from fire, heaters, hot liquids and irons.

Toddler, preschool and school-aged

Always use a car seat or seat belt. Discuss dog, street, garage, tool, water, match, fire and bicycle safety. Avoid trampolines, which may cause neck injury. Fence play areas and watch your child while in a play area. Windows in homes must be checked to be certain they are locked. Unload and put away all firearms.

Warn your child about the dangers of abduction (Ch. 3).

POISON PREVENTION

Protect your child from poisons. Accidental poisoning commonly occurs in children under five years of age. Poisoning typically occurs at specific times, usually associated with some family disruption. When there is tension, illness, marital discord, job loss or visitors, the disruption allows your child to get into things that are usually inaccessible. When children under one year are poisoned, it is usually due to someone making a mistake in giving medicine. Older children are adventuresome and curious and may experiment with products and medications. Particular areas of concern must include the kitchen, garage and play areas.

Poisonous substances in your household may include medications, dishwasher soap, cleaning supplies, drain-cleaning crystals or liquids, paints and thinners, automobile products and garden supplies. Place these substances in areas that are not accessible to your children or in a locked cabinet. Put all of these items away before you bring your new baby home. That way you won't put it off until your child is "old enough to worry about poisoning." You might forget. *Always consider the location of dangerous substances from the perspective of your child.* From this level, areas that you consider inaccessible may be easy to reach. Pay particular attention when you are visiting other homes or when you have visitors. Helpful guidelines to "poison-proofing" your house include:

1. Keep all household products, plants and medicines out of reach;
2. Store medicines in a safe place;
3. Read all product labels for potential dangers;
4. Do not take medicines in front of children. Medicines should not be referred to as "candy";
5. Discard old medicines periodically;
6. Use child-resistant, safety-closure packaging;
7. Always keep syrup of ipecac readily available.

Poison-proof your home every six to 12 months to be certain that new dangers do not exist and that you are sure that potentially dangerous items are stored in places that have not become accessible to your children as they have gained skills. For those of us who are "collectors," we all need to remember to make sure dangerous or valuable items are in the "right" place. A checklist may be valuable in surveying your home:

REDUCING POTENTIAL HOUSEHOLD POISONS

Kitchen	Household products, cleaners, etc., are out of reach Medicines are removed All containers have safety-tops.
Bathroom	Medicine chest is cleaned regularly and locked Old medicines are thrown out Medicines are in safety-top containers Sprays, perfumes, cosmetics, hair-care products and fingernail preparations are out of reach.
Bedroom	Medicines should not be kept in or on dresser or bedside table All perfumes, cosmetics, powders and sachets are out of reach.
Laundry	All bleaches, soaps, detergents, fabric softeners, etc.
Garage/ Basement	Insect sprays and weed-killers are in locked area Gasoline, car products, turpentine and paints are inaccessible.
Other areas	Alcoholic beverages are out of reach Ashtrays are empty Toxic plants are given away.

(Modified from material by the Rocky Mountain Poison Control Center, Denver, Colorado.)

Emergency management of the poisoned child is discussed in Ch. 7 and on page 182.

CHOKING PREVENTION

Avoid popcorn, peanuts, small toys and balloons because they are frequently inhaled. Choking on such items is the second greatest cause of accidental home deaths in children under four years of age. Important steps to prevent choking include:

1. Do not allow your young child to play with small objects. Children under three should not play with objects less than 1 1/4 inches in diameter. (Measuring devices exist to test the appropriateness of play items.);
2. Keep children from putting foreign objects or large pieces of food in their mouths;
3. Avoid peanuts, grapes, raisins, small pieces of hot dogs, popcorn or hard candy;
4. Keep children quiet while eating. Running, walking and other activity may increase the risk of choking on inhaled food;
5. Children can inhale a balloon either when it is uninflated or if it bursts. Be careful;
6. Children can inhale plastic bags, particularly those used for dry cleaning. Plastic bags can also cause suffocation. Make sure you keep them away from your children.

BICYCLE SAFETY

Bicycles are a common source of injuries to your child. Injuries result from using bikes incorrectly, from riding with a passenger on the handlebars, or from fitting bicycles improperly.

Purchase considerations

Fit the bicycle to your child. The seat should be no higher than your child's hip, and your child should be able to place the balls of both feet on the ground. When straddling a boy's bike with both feet flat on the ground, there should be an inch of clearance between the central bar and the crotch. The feet should reach the pedals without using blocks and arms should easily reach the handlebars. Children under five commonly use five- to six-inch wheels, those eight to ten years old use 24-inch wheels and older children can normally use 26- to 27-inch wheels.

Bicycles for younger children should have coaster brakes because hand brakes require too much strength and coordination.

Avoid bicycles with gear shift controls on the crossbar.

Infant seats should have protection from the bicycle spokes and seat belts that are sturdy and easy to operate. The weight should rest over the back wheels. Children under six months should not be carried on the back of a bicycle.

Reflectors should be on the front and rear wheels. The back reflector should be visible for 300 feet and a front headlight visible from 500 feet.

Safety helmets should always be worn. If you are trying to teach your child to ride a bicycle, use training wheels and practice in an unused parking lot. Advise your children to follow traffic signals, signs and rules. Set rules about where and when they can ride their bicycles. Have them use bicycle paths when possible and make sure they ride *with* the traffic. Avoid letting children ride after dark unless properly equipped with lights, reflectors and light-colored clothing. Sunset is the most dangerous time. Avoid riding when streets are wet, and beware of potential hazards such as grates, potholes, soft shoulders, oil spots, wet leaves and sand. Remind your children to *Be smart! Be careful! Be safe!*

All-terrain, four-wheeled vehicles have become an increasing source of injury; specific safety guidelines must be followed. They should never be used by children under 14 years of age or at night. Passengers should never be permitted and a helmet should be worn at all times. Three-wheeled, all-terrain vehicles should not be used.

WATER SAFETY

Observe and teach your children water safety. Infants and toddlers who take swimming lessons should not be considered to be water safe. They rarely have the common sense to be safely left alone near water.

Never leave young children alone in or near water or use unreliable flotation devices. Teach safe water behavior; do not permit running, pushing, jumping or diving in shallow water. Do not allow access to drugs or alcohol. Floating toys or mattresses should not be used as life preservers. Avoid glass in the pool area and keep electrical appliances and equipment away from the water. Pools should have a four-sided wall or fence at least 4 1/2 feet high. Teach your children to remain calm, tread water and float on their back until help arrives, should they swim or drift from the side of the pool and be unable to swim back.

Learn CPR (see Ch. 7).

FIRE SAFETY and ELECTRICAL HAZARDS

Fire safety starts with prevention. Protect children from obvious sources of danger:

1. Always buy flame-retardant garments as well as fabrics for furniture, drapes, etc.;
2. Store and use flammable materials properly. Never use flammable liquids near a source of flame;
3. Inspect electrical equipment periodically for defective wiring;
4. Avoid using hot vaporizers or pots to increase humidity;
5. Keep cords out of reach. Pulling over percolators, pans, iron and pots is common. Make certain all pot and pan handles are facing toward the back of the cook top;
6. Never leave your child alone in a bathtub;
7. Install smoke detectors in each sleeping area and at the head of stairways;
8. Install fire extinguishers in high-risk places;
9. Develop an escape plan and conduct drills;
10. Pay special attention to these simple but necessary precautions:
    - Store matches in child-proof container;
    - Store gasoline and combustible liquids safely;
    - Vent and locate heaters safely;
    - Vent water heater correctly and adjust thermostat to 120° Fahrenheit to prevent scalding;
    - Screen fireplaces.

OUTDOOR SURVIVAL TECHNIQUES

Review survival techniques with your children in case they get lost in a rural or mountainous area. When planning a hike, have each of your children take along a whistle, a garbage-size plastic bag with a hole for the face to provide rain protection, (suffocation is possible without the hole) and suitable clothing for protection from the weather. Teach children to stay in one place if they get lost. They should focus on staying warm, dry, and protected. A unique program teaches children to hug a tree when lost, since staying close to trees will keep them moderately dry, protected and in one place. Your children should be reminded that if they get lost, there will be many people looking for them and they should make every effort to draw attention to themselves by making crosses or other marks with trees and rocks and by making noise with their whistle.

BASIC EQUIPMENT

Car seat

Automobile-related accidents account for a large number of injuries to children; car seats provide tremendous protection if used appropriately. Not only are they protective, there is abundant evidence that improved car behavior results when children are routinely placed in their own car seat—they have a place of their own and the whole trip is easier. More than one car seat may be required to share pick-up and car-pool responsibilities.

Purchase considerations

Current standards require that infant and child restraints are dynamically crash tested. Select a car seat that is convenient and easy to use that meets all safety standards. The following aspects of car-seat design deserve consideration:

1. Harness: The five-point harness comes over the shoulders around the hips and through the legs. It does not usually require a shield or armrest for protection and is preferred. The three-point or V-shaped harness is used in infant-only seats and in those toddler seats with a shield;
2. A full shield is designed to absorb the crash forces across the entire body. A partial shield absorbs the crash forces in the lap area and must be used with a harness;
3. A tether or anchor strap may attach to the rear of the safety seat. It connects to an anchor plate which must be secured to the auto frame or rear lap belt. Incorrectly used tether straps reduce the protection provided;
4. Armrests provide no safety function and must be used with a five-point harness.

Safety tips

1. Approved (meeting or exceeding federal safety standard No. 213-80), crash-tested restraints should be in-

stalled and used correctly;

2. Always restrain children when the vehicle is in motion;

3. Children four to five years of age or over 40 pounds may use a standard lap belt worn across the hips. They should sit on a firm cushion with the back straight against the rear seat. Children under 55 inches in height should not use a shoulder strap; no one should use a shoulder strap without a lap belt;

4. Not only do children behave better in the car when accustomed to always using a car seat, they also get a better view of the scenery;

5. During warm weather, protect the frame and strap from getting too hot.

Cribs

Purchase considerations

To prevent injuries, specific safety standards have been established for cribs. Eight criteria currently exist:

1. Slats of a crib should be spaced no more than 2 3/8 inches apart to avoid neck entrapment. Be sure no slats are missing or cracked and no crossbars or toeholds are present on the sides. When the sides are fully lowered, they should reach four inches above the mattress;

2. The headboard and footboard should not have openings that permit strangulation;

3. Corner posts should be less than 5/8 inch above the railing to prevent catching necklaces or cords around the neck;

4. The mattress should fit snugly. If more than two of your fingers can fit between the edge of the mattress and the side of the crib, the mattress is too small;

5. Make certain that the bumper pad fits around the entire crib. Tie or snap it into place with at least six snaps. Discontinue use of the bumpers when your baby can pull to a standing position because at that point, your baby will use the pad to climb out of the crib;

6. Buy a crib with the largest possible distance between the top of the side rail and the mattress support;

7. Make sure your baby cannot easily release the drop-side latches and that the latches hold securely in the raised position;
8. Use only high-quality enamel paint. Make certain that there are no splinters or cracks.

Safety tips

1. If a crib is next to a window, avoid having drapery or cords within reach, since children may strangle themselves;
2. Lock the side rail in the raised position when your baby can stand;
3. When your baby reaches 35 inches in height or can climb or fall over the sides, replace the crib with a bed;
4. Periodically check the screws and bolts that secure the parts of the crib to be certain they are present and tight;
5. Gyms and brightly colored toys used on cribs to provide stimulation should have no strings longer than 12 inches, to prevent entanglement. Small parts can be a choking hazard. Attach or install toys securely so your baby cannot pull them down into the crib. By five to six months of age, or at the age your child is able to push up on hands and knees, remove crib gyms.

Playpens

Purchase considerations

1. Mesh should have openings that are less than 1/4 inch, so that buttons on clothing do not get caught;
2. For wooden playpens, slats should be no more than 2 3/8 inches apart and no more than 2 3/8 in width.

Safety tips

1. Playpens with drop-side mesh present a potential danger. When the side is left down, the mesh hangs loosely and forms a potential pocket, which your child can roll into, risking suffocation. Never put your child in the playpen when the side is down;
2. Never use a playpen with holes in the mesh sides since children can entrap themselves. The mesh must be securely attached to the top rail and the floor plate;

3. Check the top rail periodically for holes and tears since children will often use this for teething;
4. Avoid large toys, bumper pads or boxes that your child can use to climb out of the playpen;
5. Toys hung from the sides should not have cords longer than 12 inches, which may cause accidental strangulation.

Gates and enclosures

Gates are useful at the top of stairs or in open doorways. Give special care to avoid entrapment and strangulation.

Purchase considerations

1. Do not choose an accordion style or expandable type. Models with a straight top edge or rigid meshscreen are desirable since V- or diamond-shaped tops or openings are potentially dangerous.

Safety tips

1. Anchor the gate to the doorway or stairs so that it cannot be pushed over;
2. If an expanding pressure bar is used, make certain that it will resist the force exerted by your child. Install it on the side away from your child. Otherwise your child may use it to climb over the gate.

Highchairs

The majority of highchair injuries result from falls, which can be minimized by the use of a waist strap. Accidents can also result if the chair collapses or falls over.

Purchase considerations

1. Look for wide-base stability. If it is a folding chair, make certain that it has a locking device;
2. Use a sturdy, easy-to-operate and independent waist-and-crotch strap or belt every time your child is in the chair;
3. The shape and size of the feeding tray should meet your child's needs;
4. Caps or plugs should be firmly attached to any metal frame tubing to prevent choking.

Safety tips

1. Always use the restraining strap or belt as soon as your child is placed in the chair. Do not use the feeding tray as a restraint;
2. Never allow your child to stand up in a highchair;
3. Always watch your child;
4. Keep the chair away from places that your child can push off from and thereby tip the chair;
5. Chairs that attach to the edge of a table by pressure/friction require close monitoring of your child to prevent falling and possible detachment, or the table tipping.

Strollers and carriages

Purchase considerations

1. A wide base to prevent tipping is important. If the seat is adjustable to a reclining position, make certain that the stroller will not tip backward;
2. Strollers that can be folded must have a locking device to prevent accidental collapse;
3. Strollers with shopping or storage baskets should have them in a low position on the back of the stroller or in front of (or above) the rear wheels;
4. Use a strong, durable and easily operated seat belt every time your child is in the stroller;
5. Make certain the brake is secure and easy to operate. Optimally, the brake should work on two wheels;
6. Look for stroller arms designed to prevent your child from getting his/her hands caught in the wheels or stroller frame.

Safety tips

1. Make sure hands are clear when folding or unfolding the stroller;
2. Always use the seat belt;
3. Do not leave your child unattended in a stroller;
4. Do not use the stroller as a play toy.

Back carriers

Back carriers allow you to carry your child while shopping, walking or doing other activities where free hands are useful.

Carriers are often comforting to children and may be helpful in reducing colic.

Purchase considerations

1. After four to five months of age, use a framed back carrier to provide head and body support. Before this age, the soft, snuggly type of front infant carrier is most appropriate;
2. Buy a carrier that is appropriate for your baby's size and weight. When you place your baby in the carrier, check to be certain there is enough depth to support your baby's back and that leg openings are small enough to prevent the baby from slipping out but big enough to avoid rubbing on the legs;
3. Make sure the material and stitching are sturdy and washable;
4. Metal frames should have padded coverings. Check for sharp points and edges;
5. Restraining straps are essential.

Safety tips

1. Always use the restraining straps to prevent your child from standing up and falling out;
2. Check the carrier periodically to make sure material and stitching are still intact. Check for sharp points and edges;
3. When folding the joints, make sure hands are clear;
4. When leaning or stooping over, bend from the knees rather than the waist to prevent your child from falling out!

Carrier seats

Carrier seats are convenient to place your child in between meals and sleeping so they can watch their environment. They are usually made of plastic and should never replace specially designed car seats.

Purchase considerations

1. A wide-sturdy base is important for stability. The supporting devices should lock securely;
2. Nonskid feet prevent skidding. If not present, attach adhesive strips to the underside;
3. Easy-to-operate waist and crotch straps are necessary.

Safety tips

1. A carrier seat is not a substitute for an infant car seat and should never be used as one;
2. Always make certain that the supporting devices are secure;
3. Always use straps;
4. Stay close to your child when the carrier is on a table or a surface from which falls can occur. If possible avoid placing the seat on such surfaces.

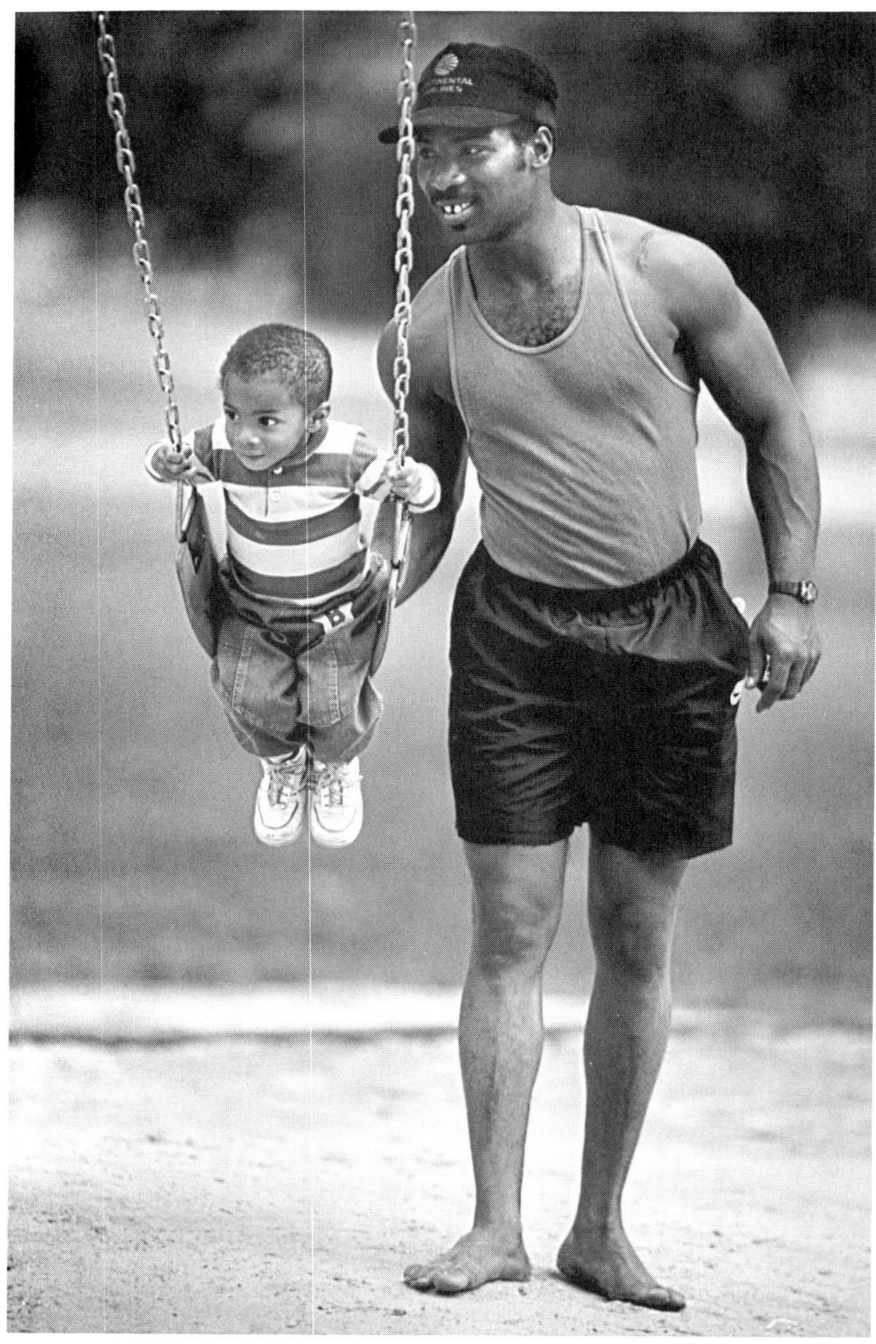

The HIGHS and LOWS of BEHAVIOR

Chapter 6

Children grow at different rates. These changes lead to behavior that is fascinating, exciting and often frustrating as you deal with new stages and new skills. The astonishing changes in behavior you will encounter are *normal* stages of *normal* development and part of the process that allows your child to become a sensitive, independent person.

In this chapter we will focus on normal development to help you understand and cope with the stages of growth you will confront. Initially we will focus on the general principles of setting behavioral limits.

GENERAL PRINCIPLES

Occasionally it is necessary to redirect your children's activity and to redefine appropriate limits. *Consistency* must serve as the basis for all such efforts. Make sure your expectations and limits are appropriate for your child's development. Don't ask your two year old to sit still at a meeting for two hours, entertain him/herself while you finish the housework, or act like an "angel" at a fancy restaurant.

Listen to, respect and give your children room for exploration, but make sure they know the limits. Be decisive when setting boundaries. Your children need reassurance and praise within this framework to allow them to develop independence while still acknowledging that there are limits that cannot be broken.

Consistent boundaries are helpful to allow your children to be secure enough to wander around and express their curiosity but also to accept the authority, love and security you provide. Without clear limits, your children won't know their boundaries and may be insecure about their relationships with adults and the environment. Although limits are good for them, don't expect them to thank you for setting early bedtime hours, using time-outs or withdrawing privileges.

Consistency and support are particularly important in helping children deal with the fear of the unknown. Your children's vivid imaginations may lead to distortion and unfounded fears. The limits you set can help structure and reformulate these fears.

Your children reflect the values and support system around them. No matter how hard you and your wife work at providing a secure environment, stress levels will vary in your home. At even the youngest age, your children will reflect any household tension and manifest their sense of discomfort and insecurity by changing behavior. Often they will become more demanding. This obviously requires action but the focus should be not only on your child but on the source of the stress. Communication between you and your children is an important part of resolving problems.

Set limits and be consistent at the same time that you are providing a positive, loving and caring environment. Be clear and concise when you define boundaries and re-establish appropriate behavior. This allows your children to feel safe.

As any father soon learns, it isn't easy to always be consistent, especially with children's constant testing of limits and attempts to circumvent the rules. However, if you remain calm and under control, you ultimately will prevail. (Even though you may have your doubts!) It is essential to maintain a sense of humor and perspective. Remember that the hard times are always followed by good ones; the converse is true as well.

Even children under a year of age understand the word "No" particularly when said in a firm voice. They respond to the communication, even if they do not understand the term. If there is no immediate response, isolation in a crib provides added emphasis. Older children clearly understand the term but tend to want to test limits and often say "No" automatically, irrespective of the nature of the request. Children at this stage say "No" to even the most tempting offers of ice cream, candy, etc., just "out of principle."

After 18 months of age, your children often need periods to cool down and think about their actions and the responses they have just endured. Adopting a quiet time is an excellent way to change behavior. This works much better than spanking or threatening since the latter approaches are short-lived and to some extent demonstrate your children's control. Always remember that you are a teacher not a policeman.

Quiet time allows your children to have time alone after unacceptable behavior, whether it is disobeying, tantrums, biting, yelling or a host of other infractions that are hard to even imagine. Both you and mom, as well as other adult caregivers, must use identical responses for similar behaviors. Define which behaviors warrant a quiet time; is the threshold for quiet time behavior such as throwing food, having a temper tantrum or biting and yelling? Develop rules; discuss the rules with everyone and clarify what is acceptable and what is inappropriate. You should discuss the rules with all of your children and explain that when there is inappropriate behavior, they will be sent to a corner of a room, a chair in the hall or some other location for a period of time. The location should be a boring place without toys, radio, television, etc. The time spent alone should be from one to five minutes depending upon the age of the child. Some people suggest one minute for children under two years and up to five minutes for five year olds and above.

Explain to your child in a calm voice what he/she has done to warrant a quiet time and send your child to the predetermined site for the specified time. Often a timer helps to reinforce the nature of the approach. If your child leaves the chair or location, the timer is reset. Once the time is up, go over and ask if your child is ready to get up. If the answer is positive, the period is over. Do not dwell on the issue anymore unless the behavior is repeated.

Remember that your expectations must be age appropriate and that most changes and variants are really normal behavior. If behavioral problems are escalating or you are getting frustrated, talk with your doctor. Rarely will professional input be necessary or appropriate.

DEVELOPMENTAL ASPECTS of BEHAVIOR

Watching your child grow is perhaps the most amazing and exciting part of raising children. Your baby is unique and during the first two years of life gains skills with a rapidity that is astounding. Each day new things are learned, new behaviors evident, and new sounds and responses present.

Part of the excitement of child rearing is that all children develop on somewhat different timetables. Although the patterns and general framework are consistent, the variability makes it fun and full of surprises.

In the course of normal development, your child will adopt behaviors that may frustrate you. Independence, separation, anxiety, and jealousy are recurrent themes that form the basis for many developmental changes that influence behavior.

Most behaviors that are considered problems are exaggerations of normal development and may be a reflection of the variability that exists among children in acquiring new skills.

Setting limits for age-appropriate risks and challenges allows your child to explore, experiment and develop self-confidence.

Newborn

Your new baby arrives with anticipation and fanfare. Quickly, you discover how much babies can interact with you and their environment. Although babies have little control of muscles and can barely (if at all) hold up their heads, they have an amazing ability to look at their environment and respond to people, sounds, colors and shapes. Talk to and play with your child, and he/she will simultaneously amuse you by gaining skills and responses.

Bonding takes place in the early weeks, creating an environment that allows you, your wife and your other children to adjust to the new family member with enthusiasm. Spend quiet time, hold your baby, play and just look; this is not only fun but allows you to share and be part of this wonderful time. Newborn babies enjoy looking at faces that are in the middle of their vision. The changes in your baby are astonishing, and you will remember these days of rapid development with tremendous fondness.

These are also days with intense time demands. There are feedings to give, diapers to change and laundry to do—chores that fill the time. Be certain that everyone is part of the excitement and is getting pleasure from the new arrival. Otherwise, there may be jealousy and rivalry generated by other family members. Relax and try to maintain some semblance of family functioning. Rigid schedules and multiple demands from neighbors, friends, work and in-laws can be a phenomenal drain.

Six weeks

By six weeks your child is increasingly able to do things and to respond in a more positive and animated way to your sounds, faces and actions. However, remember that even as a newborn, your baby was taking it all in, but just not responding. Now your child is making some sounds and smiling in response to faces that are outside the middle of his/her vision.

Although your baby still sleeps continuously, he/she is more responsive and makes more noises, in part as a response to your actions. Your baby feeds with somewhat more purpose and is less passive in terms of position and demands.

Interactive playing is essential. Your baby follows brightly colored objects better and even makes early attempts at grabbing things. However, your baby won't hold objects or play with them in a consistent manner at this time.

Four months

Your four month old is sociable and responds to your every word with an exciting array of faces, sounds and motions. Your baby squeals, coos or babbles constantly either for amusement or to get a response from someone else. Your baby responds to most people willing to play, crawl, squeal or make funny faces. Smiling becomes more common.

Muscle control improves, and there is more physical interaction with the environment. Four month olds look at their hands and grab for things. They may be able to grasp an object with a wide swing of the arms and hands, and may slowly develop an ability for self-support while being held in someone's arms or in an infant seat. One of the most exciting events is when your child turns over for the first time. Often your child does not understand what has just happened and begins to cry once this tremendous feat has been achieved. There is some evidence that children of this age enjoy being held in a standing position. Increased control allows 4-month-old babies to entertain themselves and to keep track of what is going on around them in a more active fashion. Their interest is still primarily in people.

Six months

Six month olds are constantly exploring. Eyes, fingers, hands and mouth become essential parts of this process. Everything is new and needs to be felt, looked at, tasted and chewed. Things can now be grabbed with more skill and even transferred from one hand to another. Cubes are common play toys. All of a sudden your child becomes a social being, making sounds for him/herself or anyone who will respond.

Sitting becomes an important landmark at this age and it may happen all of a sudden. Your child is in constant motion, but crawling is limited by the inability to keep the stomach off the floor.

Nine months

Interaction with the world becomes more sophisticated. Body movements become more purposeful, usually with the goal of moving toward something that appears attractive. Standing is accomplished by holding onto an object. Your baby is reaching out to learn about things, places and people. Picking up objects becomes commonplace and touching everything is universal. The index finger and thumb can now work together in an efficient pincer action, thereby expanding their world immeasurably.

Your child wants to be included in everything. Games like peek-a-boo are fun. Behavior modification becomes practical; the tone of "No" is understood. "Dada" and "Mama" as well as imitative sounds become incorporated into the language pattern.

Children listen to picture books for longer periods of time. Stranger anxiety becomes a dominant force. Parents are clearly preferred to everyone else, and your children, who a month earlier loved anyone holding them and paying attention, now cry whenever someone else picks them up. There is tremendous variability in this stage, and it will pass. It is part of a child's development toward becoming a healthy, independent individual.

Sitting is now perfected. Children scoot or crawl, permitting astounding mobility. Many children never crawl much if they have acquired efficient scooting skills. The object is to get from one place to another, not to acquire seemingly "unnecessary skills."

Twelve months

The first birthday is a landmark and walking is the big achievement, although your child may not become an efficient walker for a few more months. The pincer grasp has improved and playing with cubes and other objects is more sophisticated.

Communication skills have escalated and single words, especially "Mama" and "Dada," are clearly understood. Simple directions are understood and limit setting becomes a reality. Children are much more responsive, waving good-bye and wanting to do things by themselves. They now have the ability to walk around and find things. Feeding time is often a matter of your child wanting to hold the spoon while combining, smearing and spilling foods.

Dependency is still paramount. Although children like to do things by themselves, separation is still difficult. The security of the favorite blanket is essential. Parents often need to stay by the crib for a few minutes until their child has gone to sleep.

Mobility is essential and becomes part of a child's desire to explore and be independent, while secure in the knowledge that a loved one is nearby. Providing an area that is safe to explore can assist in this growth.

Eighteen months

The 18 month old is an explorer whose world has expanded over the last few months. Walking has opened a whole new world and, when combined with crawling, leaves no place safe from the curiosity and initiative of these youngsters. There is a tremendous sense of independence and a much greater focus on what they really want. Although separation from parents is now more acceptable, 18 month olds may frequently reassure themselves by checking to see if you are watching them.

Behavior becomes somewhat inconsistent, and your baby may develop fears of certain happenings such as baths or loud noises. Often children demonstrate their temper and displeasure with parental limits. Diverting attention to more acceptable activities is usually easy in this age group. Consistency on the part of the parent is critical to reinforce appropriate behavior patterns for children.

"No" will become an important part of an expanded vocabulary, particularly when your child's immediate desires are not met. Vocabulary increases to several other single words, accompanied by constant babbling. Words are imitated and usually one or more body parts are incorporated into normal speech.

Playing with friends is now more fun. Children will often get frustrated when they cannot do something that they want; diverting attention may be useful. Children can turn pages by themselves, and they like to draw and scribble. They can partially undress themselves at this time.

Two years

Independence is the hallmark of two year olds, who are trying to build new skills and competencies. They want to do everything themselves and get things exactly their way. They want choices, which should be given when appropriate (e.g., what clothes to wear but not when to go to bed or eat). The two year old has emblazoned the word "No" on all communications. Periodically, these intense feelings of independence do give way to a need to be held, praised and supported; enjoy these moments while they last because your child is growing up.

Your child can now move around with tremendous skill, even on a tricycle. Balls can be kicked, steps climbed and objects jumped over. Vocabulary is increasingly sophisticated, and sentences can be understood and words combined. Pictures can often be named and body parts identified.

Cooperative play and sharing remain limited. Listening to stories and helping with housework are favorite activities.

Three years

Preschoolers can pedal a tricycle and go upstairs alternating steps. They enjoy playing with blocks and can even stack them. Balls can usually be thrown overhand a small distance. Copying objects is tremendous fun. Speech is more understandable. Preschoolers can describe pictures by combining different objects and describing the action within the story.

They enjoy buttoning their clothes and can wash and dry their hands. They can begin to brush their teeth independently (but often forget unless reminded and supervised). Play is more interactive. Masturbation may occur.

Four years

Hopping is a favorite activity, and the sense of balance improves markedly. Four years olds still love to copy and imitate pictures. People increasingly become the subject of their drawings. Speech is totally understandable; describing opposites is a favorite game. Questions constantly include why, how and when, and must be recognized as important parts of the learning process.

Children can usually dress themselves with help, and many are toilet trained. Separation from parents is easier, and play groups work cooperatively.

Five to eight years

Balancing is now possible as is playing with a bouncing ball; eye-hand coordination and speed are improved. Drawings of people are more complicated, including multiple body parts. Exploring is paramount and constant. Children expect more control over their environment and exhibit greater self-reliance. They have more requests for group activities, sports and other diversions.

Language is tremendously important; vocabulary is expanded so that children know body parts and learn longer words. Numbers and letters are increasingly recognized.

Children can dress themselves.

Children in the first years of life change at remarkable speed. The early months require a supportive and nurturing environment. As your child approaches two years, the challenges change and the focus must be on providing a nurturing, supportive environment. During the preschool and school-age periods new excitement, challenges and growth are inevitable.

EATING

Food is a necessity and becomes a focus for stress in some families. For the new baby, eating is one of the major activities of child rearing. Whether it is bottle or breast-feeding, this time with your new baby is a unique chance for peace and solitude for you, mom and baby. Babies have a fantastic ability to regulate their feeding, and demand-feeding is generally preferred although limits need to be placed on the frequency. Feeding should be a joint effort for both you and mom, dividing the responsibilities as appropriate.

Feed your new baby every two to three hours; by one month of age this can be stretched to every three to four hours. Infants will usually remind you of this time frame but would prefer to eat more frequently. If permitted, your new baby would like to eat every hour or two. Don't permit this to happen for a couple of reasons. First, your baby doesn't need to eat that often. Secondly, if you feed your child that often, you and your wife will have no time to yourself and will be overwhelmed by the responsibilities of children, family and work.

With breast-fed children, a bottle feeding in the middle of the night (2:00 a.m. or so) is often very conveniently done by dad. This allows mom to rest and lets dad share some of the fun and excitement of feeding. This quiet time alone is important for everyone. The breasts easily accommodate to this routine (see page 43).

Introduce solids around six months of age. Feeding is only necessary three to four times per day with bottles given four to five times per day. Feeding solids becomes a fun time for interaction between you, mom and your child. It is a delight to watch your children feed. Your baby will learn to use his/her tongue when using a spoon and later a cup. Although messy, this is another stage in gaining independence and is fun to watch (if you don't mind cleaning up). By 12 months, your child is particular, often selecting food on the basis of texture. Development is accompanied by throwing food and utensils and being assertive about likes and dislikes.

By six to nine months of age, your child will be able to use a spoon and will be comfortable holding a bottle. Eventually a cup will be used routinely. Reduce the mess of the transition from bottle to cup by using a special weighted cup with a spout. Bottles should normally be eliminated by 18 months of age. Do not put your child to bed with a bottle; this predisposes to cavities.

As your child approaches two years of age, his/her independence escalates at feeding time and may be a constant source of confrontation. Children want to demonstrate control of their environment by not wanting to eat anything, and certainly not the foods that you think are ideal. In addition, forcing children to eat may lead to obesity later.

Do not make eating a battleground! The nutritional needs of your child are less defined at this age, leaving room for more flexibility. Children will not stay hungry for long. You must make it clear who is in charge.

If your child refuses to eat or throws food on the floor, that meal is over. There should be no between-meal snacks or other options until the next meal. Give your child tiny servings at the next meal; your child then has a choice—to repeat the previous behavior or to eat the meal and ask for seconds if still hungry. If so, they should be graciously and quickly provided. This technique should end the constant battles about food and hopefully reduce tension about eating. Stay away from power struggles!

Children often develop favorite foods; allow them to help select foods once the range of choices is clear and acceptable mealtime behavior has been established. It may be useful to feed your youngster before the family dinner, which is usually later and relatively lengthy. Your children should be allowed to join the family for dinner and conversation and have a snack or special toy.

As conflict over eating decreases, the family dinner becomes an important time to maintain cohesiveness and share experiences. Eating is a very social experience, and once many of the early control issues have been resolved, dinner can be the special time of each day that brings the family together (see "Family night," Ch. 2).

Occasionally, you may want to eat out as a family. This goes relatively smoothly with infants, but as your children get older, they have less patience for going to restaurants. Choose the right restaurant by determining the type of service, the formality of the setting and whether there are activities for children. With younger children, always remember to bring that special blanket or other object, as well as a few other diversions.

Periodically go out for a quiet evening as a "couple" and renew and strengthen your relationship.

SLEEPING

Your newborn

Your newborn spends a great deal of the day sleeping. Most children sleep through the night by three months of age, although 50 percent have some night waking during the first year. Try to have a peaceful time by reading, sitting or rocking before putting your baby to bed. If your baby does wake up at night, it is usually due to some stimulus in your environment. Commonly you pick up your baby, change the diaper and give a bottle when your child cries. Although it is natural to want to do this, this extra stimulation must be discouraged. In essence you are giving your baby everything he/she could wish for in the middle of the night; there is little or no reason to wake up at that time. What more could a baby want—the full attention of parents at a moment's notice.

Do not respond more than necessary. Changing the diaper and putting your baby back in to the crib is the response that will end night waking quickly. Let your child cry if necessary. However, other factors may also contribute. Infants should, if possible, sleep in their own room or area of the living quarters. Minimize noise and bright lights; a night light is sometimes reassuring. Separation may also create anxiety that results in sporadic waking at night; it will resolve.

Toddlers

Sleeping problems become less of an issue after one year, although there may be some transient problems. Once children learn how to crawl and climb out of their crib, they should be moved to a junior bed or a mattress on the floor.

Sleep problems are usually associated with some frightening experience that occurred before bed, whether real, imagined, viewed on the television or heard from a book. Obviously, avoid these experiences. Reading calming stories, singing or talking before bed is often useful.

The dark may be scary and a night light useful. Your children may have difficulty distinguishing fantasy from reality. This may lead to nightmares as children relive such experiences. Provide extra stability if there are sleep problems; be available during the night rather than going out and leaving your child with a baby sitter. Children may wake up with the fear that parents have left, and it is reassuring to find a parent available. Always tell children about plans to go out. Try to leave after they are asleep to avoid disrupting their routine. Surprises usually create problems!

Naps are often required early in this period but tend to diminish between two and five years of age.

Older children

Sleep requirements and problems begin to parallel those of adults. Sleep disruption is usually a response to stress. If not easily resolved, ask your doctor to help clarify possible problems.

SIBLING RIVALRY

Prepare your child for the arrival of a new sibling. Sharing you and mom does not necessarily come easily. Imagine your indignation if your wife brought home a second man to share her affections. During the last trimester, let your older children feel your new baby's movements and share in the excitement by helping to pick out clothes, choose color schemes, etc. Help your children understand some of the physical changes that are occurring. When planning for your new baby, be certain not to displace your older children. Do not change rooms, beds, baby-sitting arrangements, etc. during the one to two months before delivery. Otherwise, the clear message will be that your new baby is taking their crib or room.

Expose older children to other babies and let them go with you to routine checkups. Children often enjoy putting together albums of their own baby pictures, allowing them to understand that they were once infants as well. Discuss the delivery with them ahead of time and review the logistics for baby-sitting while you are at the hospital. Sibling preparation courses are also available at many hospitals and birth centers.

Make the delivery a moment of excitement for your children; make arrangements for a favorite baby sitter, relative or friend to care for your children when you go to the hospital. The actual birthing process is a wonderful moment and when possible should be shared by both dad and mom.

Focus your efforts on making a smooth transition. Dads play a very important role to make sure that all the children are included in the anticipation and excitement of childbirth. Once the new baby has arrived, have your children visit the hospital to see mom and baby. Allow your children to hold your new baby (with help); this can be reassuring to older children. Try to minimize separation between you, mom and your other children. Many believe that the separation of family members during this period can make sibling rivalry worse. While mom and baby are in the hospital, plan special activities for older children.

When it is time to bring the new arrival home, have a friend or family member take your older children out for another special event while you get settled. Then when your older children come home, you are settled and relaxed and can give them a big hug and a great deal of attention. It is often useful to have a gift from your new baby for each of your other children. This converts what might be a negative event into one with very positive memories. Interestingly enough, these gifts are long remembered and a frequent source of discussion at later birthdays.

Older children will often be very demanding for attention; they are clearly competing and testing. Be sensitive to these forces but maintain the limits of behavior you have traditionally established in your family. Often there will be some regression in behavior and toilet training. Acting out is common. Talk with your older children using open-ended questions such as "What do you think of our new baby?"

Over the next days and weeks, include your older children in the baby's care. Reassure your children and keep them involved while you buffer yourself and your wife from outside pressures. Make the kids feel grown-up, thereby minimizing the sense of jealousy. Your major tasks are to care for the new baby and to be certain that your other children are included in this care, demonstrating that they can all be loved. Emphasize that there is no finite amount of love and that the new baby does not mean they will be loved less.

Your new baby is demanding and time consuming. However, it is essential that you continue some of the family's earlier patterns. When mom is occupied with feeding, diapering or sleeping, focus on the older children and vice versa. Set aside time each day for reading, playing, talking, drawing or other activities. Plan special events, which can be as simple as going out to a fast-food restaurant, visiting the zoo or museum, or going to the park to play. These are long-remembered moments that become part of the family routine. When friends and relatives visit, make sure they first pay attention to your older children. If they bring a gift for the new baby, let them also bring one for your older children. (To avoid awkward moments, it is worthwhile to have a supply of gifts for your older children in case a visitor forgets.)

It is not unusual for older children to hit their new sibling. This obviously must be monitored and discouraged. Praise, support, discussion and understanding can eventually help to establish the concept that the new baby is a playmate.

During this period of transition, you too may also become jealous. Your family, and most particularly your wife, is totally focused on your new baby. You now have an unequaled rival for time, energy, love and attention. It is important to accept such feelings as natural, deal with them honestly and recognize their origin. Try to steal some protected time with your wife.

As your new baby gets older, the focus of jealousy changes direction, and attention must be given to making sure that children share. *Balance and equity between children must be the foundation of arbitrating and negotiating all conflicts.* My 11 year old was once heard making the classic statement, "It isn't fair that everything needs to be so fair." Acknowledge negative feelings about a brother or sister and discuss their envy, jealousy and resentment to put it in perspective.

Siblings rarely reach agreement on sharing, and there will be confrontations over the years. Having individual toys in separate areas as well as a combined area for joint toys may reduce friction. This allows each to have some control over prized possessions but also forces real sharing on other items. Children must learn to wait their turn and to share. There will be many times when parents will need to negotiate and arbitrate. Praise children when they share; call for quiet time and discussions after fighting. Always reinforce the specialness of each child and avoid comparisons and competition.

THUMB-SUCKING

Infants are born with a sucking reflex and quickly learn that this is a source of many positives including food and security. A newborn's desire to suck goes way beyond merely obtaining food; they would like to suck constantly.

Children quickly learn that they can suck their thumb (or several fingers) and partially satisfy their need for comfort and security. However, new babies cannot get their thumbs in their mouth and may quickly become frustrated. A pacifier (contour-shaped, blind nipple is preferable) is a useful substitute until coordination is improved. Pacifiers often quiet children. To withhold pacifiers because you do not want your child to suck anything but the nipple or bottle is probably useless; ultimately babies find their thumbs or other objects.

As your child gets older, sucking is no longer imperative for feeding and the thumb may have gotten "old"; a favorite object, such as a blanket or stuffed animal may become a useful substitute that serves as a source of security and comfort. Providing some soothing object is useful during moments of stress and when your child is tired, hungry or in a strange environment. Once committed, it is essential that such an object *always* be carried along. A major crisis invariably occurs if the blanket or stuffed animal is left home while traveling or visiting elsewhere; try not to forget these important items!

Eventually your child will grow out of thumb-sucking and requiring a favorite object, but the process may not be on *your* timetable. Unless there are specific dental issues, extended thumb or pacifier sucking should not cause problems. It is essential not to make it an issue.

Support and encourage your children to give up thumb-sucking at two to three years of age; they usually give it up by four years. Let them decide when they are ready. If they are reluctant, a reward system based on the number of days without sucking the thumb is useful. If they continue sucking past four years of age, it is usually worthwhile to have an occasional discussion about the topic and to provide a positive system of rewards to encourage thumb-sucking to stop. Reassure your child that you understand it is difficult to stop. Usually this, with praise and positive feedback is adequate, if done consistently and with enthusiasm.

Some children request help in this process, and putting a mitten on the hand at night might be useful. Or you might try a harmless but foul-tasting substance that is applied to the thumb or finger that your child ordinarily sucks. The substance is applied in the morning, before bedtime and each time any sucking occurs. When a week passes without any thumb-sucking, the morning application is stopped. The evening application stops after a second week without sucking, leaving applications only at times of observed sucking. This should be combined with a system of positive rewards, such as stars or checks on a chart designed to achieve a defined goal after a certain number of good days.

Remind your child that "Big children don't do that!" and the behavior usually ends, with occasional lapses if new stresses or changes in the environment are encountered. Do not nag.

TOILET TRAINING

When and how become the main questions as your child approaches the second birthday. Then there is the constant frustration and the third question surfaces, "Will it ever happen?" Remember, there are very few high school students who are not toilet trained; each child develops at his own pace.

Timing is the key. If you time your efforts correctly, the process will go smoothly. Bowel control usually comes between 18 months and three years of age, and bladder control follows. The training process goes most smoothly if begun after two years of age. Total night training may come somewhat later but should not be a source of worry until after five years of age. If they are ready, your children will often train themselves with only a little encouragement. If they are not ready, you are entering into a major battle which becomes a confrontation of wills. Two year olds often win.

Your role in toilet training is important. Provide constant support and praise rather than punishment, coercion or negative feedback. Encourage your children by repeatedly stressing the benefits of dry diapers in terms of comfort and that "big boys and girls use the toilet." Make sure they understand that using the toilet is how to keep diapers dry. Be consistent in terminology for urination and bowel movements such as "pee-pee" and "poo-poo," as well as "dry," "wet" and "potty."

Your children are ready when they understand how to use the toilet, have enough independence to get to the bathroom and can verbally communicate their desire to use the toilet. They should be at a stage to want to please you and cooperate. Children often want to imitate their older brother or sister (or parents). They should be able to walk to the bathroom, take off some clothing and be willing to sit on the potty chair. Read to your children while they are sitting on the potty seat. You and your wife and other key caregivers must be consistent. Toilet training should not begin when there are major changes anticipated in your family such as a new baby, change in jobs, moving, etc.

Once you are ready, put your child in cotton training pants and make it a big issue by saying, "Well, let's try now!" Have your child sit on the potty seat for five to 10 minutes while you are reading a story or doing some other fun activity. This is best done after meals and naps, at the times bowel movements normally occur or whenever there is a suggestion that your child needs to go. Repeat this several times during the day as time permits. After each session, your child should be rewarded and praised. Be good humored and casual. Dress your child in loose-fitting clothes that are easily removed. Sitting on the toilet will become more natural, and there will be a closer association between bowel and bladder control and using the toilet.

Eventually the impossible will happen; offer lavish praise and rewards from everyone so that it is clear that this is a family activity. If there is increasing resistance or no response after two to three days of this routine, it should be stopped for a few weeks until your child is more receptive. Pushing the issue too early may result in your child "holding"; constipation and abdominal pain may develop. If it does not go smoothly the first time and your child is under two years of age, wait until after the second birthday and then try again. Each time training is attempted it will get a little easier and you can build on the previous experience. If you are not successful after several tries or you are getting increasingly frustrated, discuss other approaches with your doctor.

There will be accidents; don't make them into major confrontations. Be supportive by saying, "Accidents do happen! Keep up the good work." Bed-wetting may continue past age five and is still common up to seven years of age.

Children who are toilet trained and begin to wet or soil

usually are responding to some stress if they are otherwise well. Have your physician rule out any medical problems, then begin to look at what problems might be bothering your child.

SCHOOL

Preparing for preschool

Entry into preschool is a major developmental phase for you and your children. This is an important part of the socialization process, as well as a period of transition for you in accepting the broader orientation and experience of children. Preschool also reduces baby-sitting requirements. By three children should have substantial involvement with peers; optimally this begins earlier.

Throughout the early years, children demonstrate a balance between independence and dependence, the latter often being no more than a rare look to a parent or a well-known baby sitter. Preschool does not usually provide this close, consistent relationship.

Your child will usually be very successful at making you feel guilty. Be firm and committed to having your child attend preschool. Do not prolong farewells. Recognize that seeing your child crying from the window with a weak wave is a hard thing to deal with every morning but is part of the process of growing up and separating from you. However, do make certain that the preschool meets your child's needs and is providing quality care and nurturing.

As you consider kindergarten, it is essential to make certain that your child is ready. Children should have an attention span that allows them to finish simple tasks such as cut and paste, and be able to understand limits and the importance of sharing with other children. Your child should also be able to share your time and the teacher's time with other children. Language skills should be appropriate. If you anticipate any problem, be honest with the teacher so that you can work on strengthening your child's skills together.

The first day of school

Whether it is the first day for a child just entering school or the beginning of a new semester, it is important to recognize this as a period of tremendous stress and tension. Children will test peers and teachers, and each year there is a new socialization process that a class goes through. Sometimes the first day goes smoothly and your child is quickly acclimated to the new classroom, teacher and group. Other times your child will remain aloof, indicating that some time is needed. Don't be disappointed; be supportive and positive.

Preparation may help. Visit the school before it opens, particularly if it is new to your child, and arrange play groups with classmates to minimize the insecurities and frustrations that are part of starting something new.

School

Parents must play a pivotal role in the educational process. Encourage children to have a positive attitude toward school. Let them blossom and grow. Make certain that you remain in good communication with teachers and that you attend conferences and give input.

Optimally, children develop a closeness and bond with their peers; help your child form such links. These relationships can be fragile and may be threatened when children are excluded from activities such as parties or trips. Try to be sensitive to this when planning events. Every child is unique; however, being different or left out can be devastating.

A unique insight may be derived from a class of third graders at Graland Country Day School in Denver who described the attributes that make them feel good about themselves:

I'm honest.
I do well.
I help around the house.
I make somebody else feel good.
I do my homework for the whole week in one night.
I clean my room.
I help someone.
People compliment my work.
I make a new friend.
I knew something that someone else didn't know.
I do excellent in something.
I finish something hard or long.
I talk to someone about my feelings.
I tuck my sister or brother in bed.

I make someone happy.
I conquer something hard.
I discover something.
Someone thanks me.

The group also described people they particularly liked as a person who:

Gives me hugs.
Can talk about anything.
Is thoughtful.
Listens to me.
Is not mean.
Likes me.
Does not walk off while I'm talking.
Is easy to make a friend of.
Shares.
Is not selfish.
Is honest.
Likes to play games.
Is nice to other people.
Is friendly to me.
Doesn't get me in trouble.
Doesn't try to show off and get me embarrassed.
Does something good for me.
Treats my things with good respect.
Is a friend.

As your children get older, establish rules about homework and other activities. Usually homework should take precedence. Most teachers try to gauge the amount of homework given to the age group being taught. If you feel it is excessive, discuss it at school. Encourage a period of reading each day. Consider setting limits on television or other diversions.

School phobia

Children may want to miss school for a variety of reasons. Vague symptoms such as abdominal pain, headache or tiredness may be the alleged reasons but are often a response to stress. Complaints usually disappear after school, during fun activities and on weekends. The problems usually result from your children being fearful of school in response to such factors as a strict teacher, potential conflicts with peers or fear of failure.

Once the pattern is apparent, it is essential that your children go back to school. There should be no exceptions to attendance, and this expectation should be specifically discussed. Discuss feelings and fears in a supportive and nonjudgmental manner, since there is usually some stress or event that is the basis of the problem. Maintain close contact with the school to monitor attendance. The school nurse should be involved in these discussions, since your child may develop symptoms during the day and should not be allowed to come home. Your child may lie down for 15 minutes and then return to class. If there are any medical reasons for your child to stay home, contact your doctor. Encourage your children to participate in activities that involve peers outside of school such as soccer, baseball or scouts.

With firmness and understanding on your part, your children can achieve a positive attitude toward school attendance. Share school activities with your children, encourage reading and participation and emphasize the fun of learning. School is a source of both education and socialization and must be part of the daily routine.

KEEPING your CHILDREN BUSY

As your children grow and mature, it is essential to develop diverse groups of age-specific activities that provide meaningful interaction between you and them. Many communities have weekly or monthly newspapers or other publications that summarize local activities. Reading together is always an option.

Play is an ideal way to entertain and occupy children, as well as to educate and socialize them. Its nature changes as your children grow, but it continues to mold your children's growth and development while strengthening the bond of love and caring.

Check all activities and toys for safety. Excellent toys are available on the market or can be made at home. Advertising campaigns have become an important force in determining children's desires; they should be monitored. Many toys indicate the appropriate age for their use; these guidelines are usually valuable. In general, avoid small objects that can be swallowed, as well as those with sharp edges or those made with potentially toxic materials (See Ch. 5).

An increasing array of activities have evolved for young children. These include aerobics, swimming, exercise and special programs for children and tots. It is essential that the primary focus is on having fun with your child; these are unique opportunities to have time during which you and your child interact without interruptions. Select programs that provide a supportive, upbeat theme that is designed to build self-esteem and foster parent-child interaction.

Newborns and babies

Although new babies spend most of the day sleeping or eating, they will soon be interested in watching, following, grasping and holding. Mobiles, dangling crib toys, cuddly objects and bath toys are appropriate. These types of toys are particularly easy to make. As babies get older, they become interested in hanging bells, music boxes and mirrors, followed by soft animals, teething toys, rattles and squeaking toys. Encourage babies to play with toys in the center of their line of vision. Reaching for objects is quickly followed by playing with blocks, different shapes and pull toys, as well as playing imitation and pattycake games.

Make reading an important part of the day. Infants love to hear rhythms and songs. Initially they are responding primarily to the rhythm. Children like to go for strolls and rides and watch things move by. They are easily kept busy by playing with people.

Toddlers

Toddlers like to do new things and try new skills. They like to explore, feel, take apart and put together. Provide your toddler with acceptable outlets and positive redirection. Applaud and praise all efforts. Blocks, magnets, water play and boats for the bathtub are terrific. As they get more sophisticated, toddlers enjoy finger-painting and drawing. They also enjoy dolls and soldiers, lacing frames, sandboxes, simple puzzles and pull trains. Try to maximize safety.

Play with peers becomes more positive and increases socialization. Children become more sophisticated in the types of trips they like. Excursions should usually be active such as going to a petting zoo or a children's museum specifically designed for touching, feeling and smelling.

Reading is crucial during this age period. Books and puzzles should be a major focus of quiet times for the family, pointing out pictures in books and eventually attempting to relate words to pictures.

Preschoolers

Activities expand rapidly and children become more interested in interactive play with peers. A variety of programs, including gymnastics,swimming and dancing are available for this age group. The key to selecting these is your child's interest and assurance that the time is spent allowing you or your wife to play, learn and interact with your child. What a wonderful chance to be together without interruption. Play groups, trips and visits with friends become very positive events and assist in many components of development. Children develop some gauges for their own behavior, making parental modification of undesirable behavior easier.

Activities for this age group include drawing, painting, printing, making collages and water play. Toys include punching bags, Play-Doh, magnets, nonelectrical trains, building blocks, dolls, chalk, clay and construction sets. Making things in the kitchen often becomes a particular source of pride. Tricycles and bikes are often introduced, and safety rules must be outlined (Ch. 5).

Reading to children is essential.

Television should be restricted.

Activities that are fun and well received are almost unlimited. Trips to the zoo or a museum are great. Children may also be interested in going to a movie that is appropriate for their age.

School-aged children

School becomes the center of activities. Many family activities evolve from a variety of interests and discoveries made at school. Many times children have a real desire to pursue these interests at home. Encourage this expansion of the school world and try to incorporate community exploration with topics that are being talked about at school.

Toys become more specific and increasingly reflect the interests of your children. Painting, building and creating are a major focus. Building things with tools, paper, cloth or other materials is fun but should be supervised for safety reasons as well as to avoid frustration. Children may also like to grow vegetables either inside or out.

Often children like animals, and a variety may be considered including dogs, cats, fish, turtles and birds. Children should assume some responsibility for their pets.

Activities may range from the simple trips mentioned earlier to more complex activities, including hiking and fishing trips; team sports such as soccer, basketball, tennis and football, ballet, gymnastics, or music and voice lessons. Serious competitive sports should normally be avoided at least until 9 to 10 years of age (if not later). Younger children may participate in such activities, but the focus should be on reaffirming the values of cooperation, good sportsmanship and sharing. Religious school may also be incorporated at this time.

Rules should be established for television viewing. Limitations should cover the amount of time spent and the type of shows watched. Programs with sex or violence should be avoided, since children under age seven have difficulty distinguishing between reality and fantasy. There are many excellent shows for children including *Sesame Street* and *Mister Rogers*.

Summer activities may include overnight camps or day camps with a variety of playmates.

Reading

Reading is a joint venture between school and home. Create an environment that allows your children to learn how to read and love it. Read to your children after work or during free moments; this builds a love for reading and learning and an appreciation for the ideas that books convey. Help children to listen and improve their language skills. Use reading time as a quiet time for you and your children.

Strengthen reading skills by applying certain principles, keeping in mind your children's ages and reading abilities:

1. Start reading to your children at an early age and set aside a time each day to be sure it becomes a part of the daily routine;
2. Start with picture books and vary the length and subject matter. Make sure they are appropriate for your children's ages. Occasionally read a difficult book to chal-

lenge but not frustrate your children;
3. Deciding whether a book is age appropriate or difficult. The "rule of fives" is useful, meaning that if there are five words on a page that are too hard for your child, the book is probably too difficult;
4. Always carry a book with you to read during boring periods or while waiting at the store, doctor, etc.;
5. Make the book interesting; read with expression and enthusiasm. Don't select a book once the plot is known, since much of the interest is lost from the start. Young children, however, love the repetition of an old, familiar story. Reading develops good listening skills;
6. Periodically stop and ask questions in a positive way about the content;
7. When it is time to stop reading, stop at a good or suspenseful spot to maintain enthusiasm for continuing the next day;
8. Limit diversions. Don't try to compete with television. A better approach is to say that the television goes off at at an age-appropriate time. At that time, your child can either choose going to sleep, reading or listening to a story in bed.

Develop activities that encourage reading skill, and also build a love for reading. Traditional approaches to reading and being read to are effective for older children. For younger children, the following may be useful:

1. Share reading with your child. Take turns reading paragraphs or periodically leaving out a word and asking your child to supply the word;
2. Build creativity into the process by having your child play one of the parts in the book and read all of that character's parts. Supplying a new ending for the story is also fun;
3. When driving or shopping, have your child read the signs;
4. Choose a letter and name all the things that begin with that letter;
5. Read the directions on game boards;
6. Write letters to your child;
7. Cut out age-appropriate cartoons and cut them apart

into sections. Have your child rearrange them to make a story;

8. Attend the children's story hour at the library or local children's bookstore;

9. Read together as a family either aloud or silently several times a week.

Reading is a tremendously important part of acquiring good learning skills and can help your children develop insight into the world beyond their immediate environment. Reading expands the imagination and gives your children a sense of creativity that should be encouraged and cultivated. A positive approach at home combined with specific activities builds a love for reading that leads to good long-term habits.

Television

Television is a mixed bag but can add to your children's exposure and enrichment if used within appropriate limits. Excellent programs, such as *Sesame Street, Electric Company* and *Mister Rogers* are available, exposing children to a wide range of people, lifestyles and noteworthy events. However, television is a passive activity, which contributes to developing children's expectations that they do not need to be creative and imaginative to be entertained. Violence is abundant, bad language is plentiful and value systems portrayed may not be in tune with your own.

To make television a positive factor in your family, certain rules may be useful:

1. Choose quality shows without violence, profanity or sex;
2. Set specific limits on the amount of time per day that your children can watch television. One to two hours per day is generally an upper limit, especially for school-age children. Exclude certain times such as meals, during homework, etc.;
3. Do not resort to television for "baby-sitting" purposes or to simply pass time;
4. Put television advertising into perspective;
5. Discuss television shows after your children watch them to make certain that they are not misinterpreted;
6. Watch special shows with your child.

Television can have a positive impact on your child if you control, restrict and focus its use. Be firm, consistent and set a good example.

The activities you plan for your children must reflect their ages and interests. They must also be realistic in terms of your availability to chauffeur. Maintain a level of commitment that provides consistency and a routine for your children's involvement. Reading can be fun, educational and a tremendous source of socialization. It also provides a fun family time. Play is your children's work; MAKE IT FUN!

CHORES and ALLOWANCES

As children grow, it is essential that they develop a sense of responsibility for specific chores within the family. These tasks must be age appropriate and reasonable. They must be fairly divided among all siblings.

Typical chores should change as your children get older. Jobs may initially include putting toys away and straightening up their rooms. Later, tasks should involve clearing the table and washing dishes. Older children may be responsible for shoveling the path, cutting the lawn, raking leaves, etc. These responsibilities must be combined with praise.

Allowance is an important component of teaching your children the value of money, and many parents combine this with completion of chores. Five and six year olds begin to understand the value of money and need to have freedom in deciding how they use it. Otherwise, your children will never learn how to make independent decisions about buying things. They need to learn that they must give up a limited resource—money—to buy things. Establish some ground rules to provide limits on what may not be purchased, such as toy guns or excessive amounts of candy. Some parents do not feel that an allowance should be tied to chores and view the allowance as solely focused on teaching the value of money. Either approach is fine.

MOVING

Moving is a stressful time for children as it is for adults.

Discuss the reason for the move with your children if they are old enough. This is particularly important if a couple is separating or getting a divorce (see Ch. 3).

When possible have your children accompany you when you are looking for a new house or apartment. Let them get to know the new neighborhood, whether the move be around the block or across the country. Involve them in the move and let them pack their most important things to reassure them that their possessions will be at the new house. Don't throw stuff away at this point; children need the security of familiar items.

Children worry about going to a new school and not having any friends. When possible, visit their new school before you move and meet the teacher. Neighbors or friends will often introduce them to children their age and give them a sense of belonging. Take every opportunity that comes up!

If the move is long distance, try to make it a fun and exciting trip but one that is restful enough so that you do not arrive exhausted.

When you get to your new house, set up your children's rooms first. Encourage friends to involve your children in activities and try to get them involved with teams or clubs.

A big move is stressful for everyone, and it is essential that the family adjust to the new community. Otherwise, it will be a hard process and your children will become incorporated more slowly into peer groups. If possible, don't get immediately involved with overwhelming responsibilities at work; give everyone a chance to adjust. Depending upon flexibility, either you or mom should ideally delay starting work until your children are adjusted to their new schools or child care, to assure your availability.

TRAVEL

Traveling with children can be a terrific family activity that provides adventure and a time to reaffirm the cohesiveness and communication that may periodically be lost with the pressures of work and home.

Decide what you enjoy doing as a family, what kinds of activities are appropriate for your children, and whether you and your wife need some time alone or whether this should be a family vacation. Try to make hotel reservations in advance if you anticipate problems making arrangements on arrival. Make certain that they can accommodate your children. Many hotels allow young children to stay in the parents' room without additional charge, making family vacations much more affordable. Decide which activities are not appropriate for children, then arrange for a baby sitter or decide that you will do those things on your next trip when the children are older or when you are alone. Sometimes, taking along your favorite baby sitter is the ideal solution.

Preparation is essential. Review plans with your children so there are no surprises. Prepare a bag of toys, books and other items for each child. Include several small new toys that will be a surprise. Bring along snacks and foods that do not melt, as well as an adequate supply of clothing, diapers (with towelettes, safety pins, plastic bags), formula, or whatever else is needed. Include special blankets or stuffed toys and a night light. Pack a first-aid kit including a thermometer, aspirin or acetaminophen (Tylenol, Tempra, etc.), tape and Band-Aids, insect repellant, sun screen and tweezers, as well as items specifically recommended by your doctor. The time of day you will be traveling should be determined by your children's routines, and environmental issues such as excess heat when traveling by car in the summer.

Airplane travel requires extensive planning but can go smoothly with preparation. Give the airline prior notice that you will be traveling with children and order special children's meals. The bulkhead is usually preferred for shorter trips because of the increased room. Get to the airport with plenty of time to be organized and avoid rushing; board early. Pack snacks, games and favorite items to be carried on board; everything else should be checked through. Pack extra clothes in case of accidents. Try to pick a time when the plane will not be full, optimally during daylight hours. Discuss ear popping, using chewing gum or yawning. When traveling with infants, let your child suck on a bottle during descent.

Children can travel alone, but arrangements must be made well in advance with the airline. Try to make it a nonstop flight. Recheck all arrangements several times and be certain that someone will be available to pick up your children when the plane arrives. Allow yourself plenty of time before the flight, since many children find the separation traumatic. Often the flight attendant can be helpful. Give your children identification and phone numbers to call in case of problems. Reaffirm that they should not talk to strangers and that if there are problems they should go to one of the uniformed airline employees. Stay by a phone until you are certain that your children have arrived. Similar arrangements can be made with interstate bus and train lines.

Traveling can be tremendous fun. Adequate preparation makes it that way.

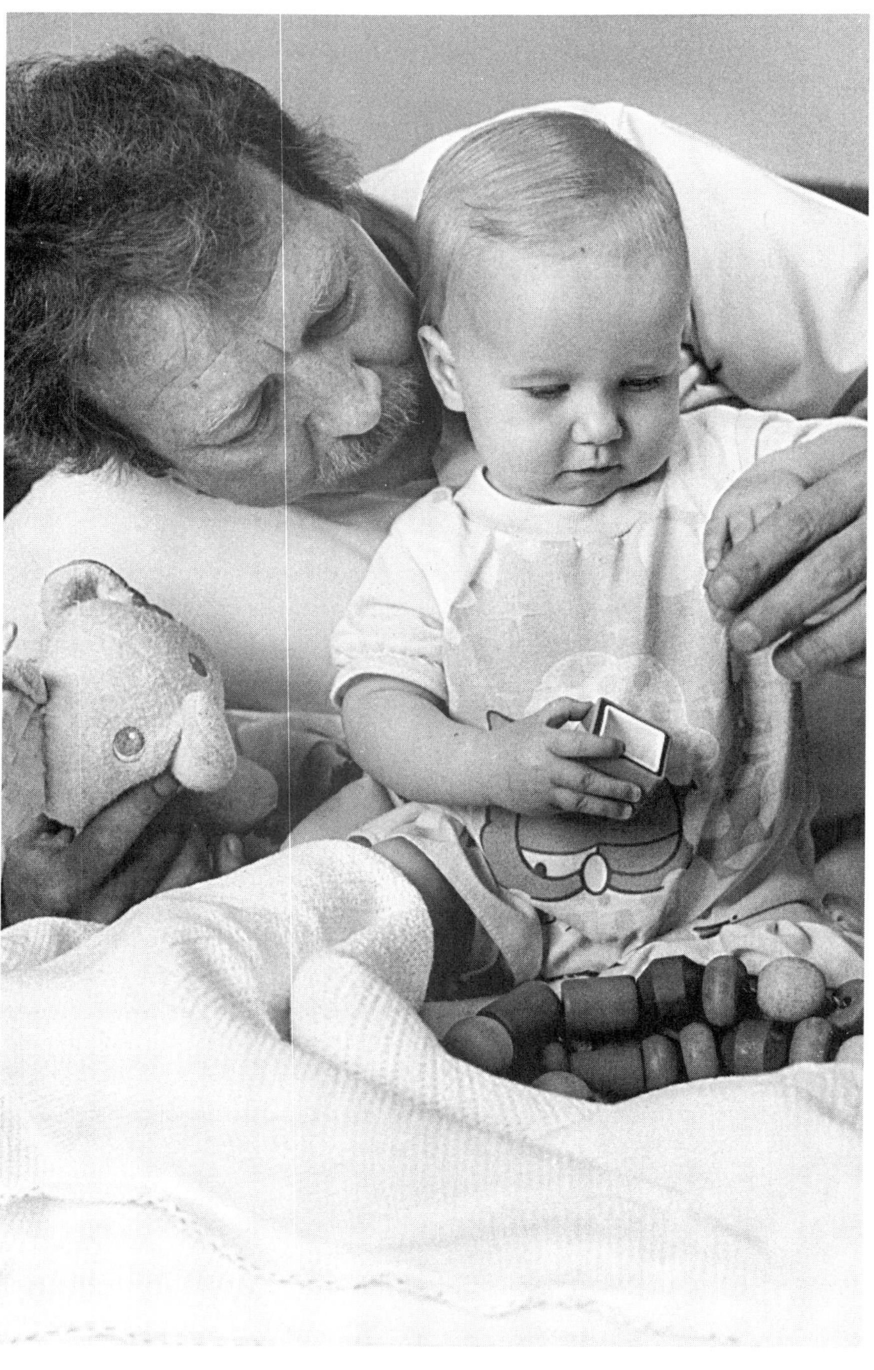

IF

YOUR CHILD

IS

SICK

Chapter 7

Unexpectedly, your children may develop medical problems. This often causes a great deal of anxiety, especially when it occurs in your infant or toddler. It is crucial that you recognize when there is something wrong with your child and when you need to get professional help in caring for your child. You need to know how to handle such problems initially, until you contact your physician or, in the case of an emergency, the 911 system.

The vast majority of illnesses require supportive care at home, often including medication and other measures suggested by your doctor. Periodically, conditions require emergency care. You should be prepared for such circumstances. Specific aspects of the illness or any underlying illness may increase the urgency of seeking medical care. Common problems may occasionally require immediate help.

If you are concerned, worried or fearful about your child's condition, it should be handled immediately. Never feel badly about asking for help if you are concerned.

The purpose of Chapters 7, 8 and 9 is to equip you with information about a number of common medical problems, so you are better able to help your child.

The section for each illness begins with a description of the illness, followed by a brief outline of what to look for and what you can do to help. There are also pointers on when you should call for help—an emergency rescue service (often 911) or your doctor—immediately, within a few hours or by appointment. If something about your child's problem concerns you, call for advice rather than sit at home worrying. Whenever you contact your doctor or other health-care provider, make certain you have the following information available:

1. Your name;
2. Phone number;
3. Child's name and age;
4. Long-term medical problems and medications, if any, and
5. A two- or three-sentence description of the present problem, including when it began, what signs and symptoms are present (particularly those that worry you), the length of the illness, its progression and any potential exposures or incidents related to the illness.

Mention if your child has a fever, a decrease in appetite or activity, an increase in listlessness or irritability, diarrhea or vomiting. Make sure you tell your doctor if your child looks "very sick."

If your child is feverish, it is usually helpful to take your child's temperature before calling and know when the last dose of fever medicine (aspirin or acetaminophen) was given and how much.

IF YOU BELIEVE IT IS an EMERGENCY, SAY SO!

Often you will need to recontact your doctor should new findings develop, the condition worsens or any problems appear that worry you.

Telephone contact can be reassuring and provide you with additional information about how to treat your child at home. Suggestions of what you can do at home fall into two basic categories—those begun by you and those requiring evaluation and initiation by your doctor. In many cases you will use both approaches.

Under some circumstances, you may need to visit your doctor. To better prepare you and your child for this, Chapters 7, 8 and 9 give you information about what to expect, outlining specific aspects of the history and physical examination, as well as procedures. As you become more knowledgeable, you will be in a better position to anticipate the components of the visit and will be prepared to be supportive when necessary.

Visiting the doctor can be a frightening experience for your child. It really doesn't matter whether the cause for the visit is something as simple as a throat culture or something more serious requiring hospitalization. It can be a big worry for a small person; their fantasies are usually worse than reality. Parents can be of great help to your children.

1. Whenever possible, prepare your children in advance. Let them know what to expect;
2. Listen to your child's questions and concerns and respond honestly;
3. Stay with your child whenever possible, to provide support, comfort and security;
4. Select care providers who are not only medically excellent, but "in touch" with your child's emotional needs;
5. Provide opportunities for your child to hear about doctors. Encourage them to play out their own experiences using dolls and stuffed animals as "patients."

During your visit, make sure that you ask questions and feel comfortable with the answers. Doctors, in the midst of a busy schedule, may not always spontaneously answer all of your questions to fully satisfy and clarify your concerns and fears. Make certain that you understand what illness your child has and what the treatment plan is before leaving the office. Otherwise, you may not feel comfortable about watching your child for changing conditions.

Remember, you are your doctor's assistant at home. You will be implementing whatever treatment is suggested and watching your child for changing signs and symptoms that may require a reevaluation.

Cautions are provided to emphasize certain aspects of the illness and to ensure that certain things are avoided that might be harmful to your child.

IF YOUR CHILD NEEDS to BE HOSPITALIZED

Although hospitalization is rarely needed, prepare yourself and your child for the possibility. Thinking about hospitalization and illness when your child is well makes it easier to handle this frightening experience should it ever be necessary. Many of these approaches may also help you prepare for a doctor's visit.

When your child is young, have him/her visit a hospital. You should visit the playroom, a child in a room and relatively threatening areas. Many hospitals have formal programs and tours to facilitate this introduction.

When hospitalization is recommended for your child, you will need to fine tune this process. The amount of preparation will reflect the urgency of the admission, but optimally there is sufficient time to prepare systematically.

Parents need to get ready first. You must feel comfortable with your decision to hospitalize your child, as well as with your doctor and the hospital. Your child may have many questions that you should be able to answer:

1. Are there preadmission tours?
2. What are the facilities like?
3. What are the rules about visitors?
4. What are the rules about rooming in for parents and siblings?
5. Can your child bring toys, clothes, family pictures and

other important and reassuring items?
6. Is there a playroom?
7. Can you arrange for a television in the room?
8. If the hospitalization is to be extended, are there provisions for school?

It is also essential to find out from your doctor what to expect. What procedures, tests, etc., will be needed? Will there be other doctors caring for your child? Who will they be?

Your child can then become the focus of the preparation process. Discuss why hospitalization is necessary. Make sure your child understands that he/she is not going to the hospital because of bad behavior but to make him/her better. Preadmission tours, books about going to the hospital, playing with doctor "toys" and perhaps talking to a child who has recently been in the hospital are all useful. Discuss the hospital in terms of what your child will see and hear; be concrete about things so that your child will understand where he/she will eat, sleep, go to the bathroom, etc. Ask your child to describe what he/she thinks is going to happen.

It may also be useful to ask questions after reading a book about going to the hospital: What do you think the child in the story thought and felt about going to the hospital? Why did they do tests like X-rays? What do you think the child thought about staying overnight? What do you think the child thought about going home?

Acknowledge your child's feelings and fears. Your child is probably scared of the hospital, its people and separation from you. Often rooming in (staying with your child) can alleviate some of the anxiety. Be simple and honest in your answers and discussions. Before leaving for the hospital, have your child help pick things he/she wants to take.

Hospitalization is stressful for you and your children. It is important for you to have someone to whom you can verbalize your own fears to help you to be supportive of your child. Throughout, try to give your child choices. Many things are determined by your child's medical condition, so let your child participate in choices such as what book to read, what program to watch, which arm to put the intravenous tube in, etc. This increases your child's participation in his/her care and reduces passivity.

There is excitement and relief when your child is ready to go home from the hospital. Try to make sure there are no disappointments; be ready for some regression of behavior once your child gets home. (If hospitalization is prolonged, regression may occur in the hospital.)

Preparing yourself and your child for the difficulties of hospitalization can make it somewhat easier for everyone.

Books that may be helpful include:

The Berenstein Bears Go To the Doctor by S.J. Berenstein, Random House, New York, 1981.

Why Am I Going to the Hospital? A Helpful Guide to a New Experience by Ciliotta C. Livingston, Lyle Stuart, Inc., Secaucus, New Jersey, 1981.

The Hospital Book by J. Howe, Crown, New York, 1981.

Eric Needs Stitches by B. R. Marino, Harper Jovanovich, New York, 1979.

My Doctor by H. Rockwell, Macmillan, New York, 1973.

A Hospital Story by S. B. Stein,Walker, New York, 1974.

Elizabeth Gets Well by A. Weber, Crowell, New York, 1970.

PREPARING for EMERGENCIES

Your child may become ill unexpectedly. Nothing is more frightening than facing a medical emergency. Although emergencies are rare, you must be able to handle them until you are able to contact your physician or the 911 system.

You can do a number of things to prepare yourself should your child have an emergency. First, determine what facilities are available in your community. During a routine visit with your doctor, discuss who and where to call. Define how to access your community's emergency rescue system. Your children's doctor is the focal point of caring for your family. Hospital emergency departments are becoming more sensitive to the special needs of children and are developing waiting and examining areas that are oriented toward children, as well as educational material to help you understand your children's problems and treatments.

Prepare an emergency card with important information and keep it on the refrigerator or next to the phone. This will be helpful for you and your family as well as baby sitters and visitors. The card should contain:

Your name ______________________________

Address ______________________________

Home phone ______________ Work ______________

If your house is difficult to find, include directions to your house and be certain that the house numbers are visible from the street. ______________________

____

____

____

Children's names and ages ______________________

____

____

____

Rescue squad phone (commonly 911) ______________

Fire department phone ______________________

Children's doctor ______________________

Phone ______________________________

Emergency department phone ______________

Poison control center phone ______________

Comments ______________________________

____

____

Other useful numbers may include your pharmacy, the names and phone numbers of close friends and neighbors, and a way to contact you if you leave your children with a baby-sitter. This information is particularly important when you have baby sitters who are new to your community.

Learn to respond to emergencies in a calm and orderly fashion. *Action is always better than doing nothing*. Stay calm, cool and collected until you can get help. Panicking only limits your effectiveness. Taking a CPR course is helpful.

Syrup of ipecac, acetaminophen (Tylenol, Tempra, etc.) for pain or fever, a thermometer, scissors, medicine dropper and bulb syringe should be available at home. Other supplies should include bandages, dressings, gauze, antibiotic ointment, an elastic roll bandage and a splint (plywood or rolled-up magazine can be used). A cool-mist vaporizer is a useful piece of equipment.

Prevention is a crucial part of your approach to preparing for emergencies.

Never feel badly about asking for help if you are concerned.

Do not try to handle things yourself; call for help. When you do call, be clear and distinct by defining the problem. For example:

"My baby is not breathing or has no heartbeat. (State the problem briefly.) My phone number is ______________."

Evaluate and treat your child as outlined in the following pages until help arrives or until you get to the doctor.

Another aspect of preparing for emergencies is providing authorization for treatment of your child in case of your absence. This is particularly important if you are out of town. There is tremendous variability in the content of authorization forms. Below is an example you may want to leave with a caregiver:

AUTHORIZATION FOR TREATMENT

I (*your name*) parent/legal guardian of (*your child's name*), a minor born (*your child's birth date*), do hereby authorize (*your caregiver at the time)* as my agent to consent to any medical or surgical diagnostic tests, procedures, treatment and hospitalization that is deemed advisable and rendered under the supervision of a licensed physician selected by my agent.

I authorize said physician or hospital providing such diagnostic and therapeutic intervention to surrender physical custody of such minor to my agent upon completion of the treatment.

This authorization shall remain effective until (*the date*) unless revoked at an earlier moment in writing to said agent or by destruction of this authorization.

Signed ______________________________________

(Parent/guardian) Date ______________

(Notary or witness optimally required to verify signature)

PROBLEMS REQUIRING IMMEDIATE ACTION

Throughout chapters 7, 8 and 9, certain conditions are listed that require immediate intervention. Just as it is important to know when not to worry and what steps you can begin at home for common problems, it is equally important to know when to worry and when your child has a problem that requires you to act quickly and call for emergency help (usually 911).

A few conditions are particularly worrisome when found accompanying symptoms of common problems. We will briefly focus on them to give you an understanding of their causes:

Blueness

Blueness or cyanosis is present when the lips, tongue or skin are blue. This problem is usually due to either heart or lung problems. In contrast, children may have blueness of the toes or fingers due to nothing more than being cold.

Difficulty breathing

Difficulty breathing, shortness or breath, or very rapid breathing occurs with abnormally excessive movement of the chest or belly or an inability to catch one's breath. Blueness may be present. This is most commonly due to a lung or airway infection or a foreign body.

Poor responsiveness

Poor responsiveness, marked lethargy, listlessness or irritability occur when children don't respond when you talk to them or ask them to do some ordinary activity. This may be accompanied by problems with breathing. Children may also be difficult to console or quiet. A serious infection, overdose of drugs, loss of water or severe injury can cause this.

Loss of water

Loss of water or dehydration is usually due to vomiting or diarrhea. Dehydrated children urinate less frequently and have fewer wet diapers (either in frequency or degree). Your child may be irritable or less active, have fewer tears and a dry mouth.

Seizures

Seizures or convulsions occur when a child has rapid jerking movements of the arms or legs. The movements usually last only a few minutes and may be due to an infection, drug overdose or head injury. The most common cause, however, is just a high fever, and in this case the seizures are usually harmless.

Remember, all of these problems require action; call for emergency help (911).

IF YOUR CHILD STOPS BREATHING (RESUSCITATING YOUR CHILD)

Although it is rare for children to require emergency care, when it does happen, it is commonly due to breathing difficulties from worsening lung or airway problems. Heart problems may then develop.

What is Cardiopulmonary Resuscitation? (CPR)

C is for cardiac, meaning heart (heartbeat);

P is for pulmonary, meaning lungs (breathing);

R is for resuscitation (bringing back the heartbeat and breathing).

The lungs breathe and draw oxygen into the blood. Oxygen is essential for our bodies to function. The heart then pumps the blood (with oxygen) from the lungs to all parts of the body. The two work together; if one stops, the other will quickly fail.

CPR temporarily supports the function of the heart and lungs until they resume functioning. It involves initiating the ABCs.

The ABCs

To successfully resuscitate your child, you must follow a very specific order of actions. Forgetting to do things in the following order can make all of the efforts useless:

A*irway:* Provide an open airway, for air to move into the nose, mouth and lungs. This can often be done simply by repositioning the head.

B*reathing:* Breathe if the child is not doing so adequately.

C*irculation*: Assist in pumping blood throughout the body.

Steps of CPR

1. *Determine Unconsciousness.* The child does not wake up or respond when shaken. In rare circumstances when a child is having difficulty breathing, yet is conscious, CPR can be life-saving.

2. *Call for help.* Determine if anyone else knows CPR and have someone call a rescue squad—usually by calling 911 or emergency number in your area.

3. *Position the child* on his/her back, lying on a firm, flat surface. This must be done with great care. If there is any head or neck injury, move the child with the head and neck firmly supported so that the head does not roll, twist or tilt.

DETERMINE IF THE CHILD IS UNCONSCIOUS

▼

CALL FOR HELP

▼

POSITION THE CHILD

(Lying on back on firm, flat surface)

4. *Open the airway.* If the child is unconscious, the tongue may block the airway or there may be mucous, blood, vomit or foreign material in the mouth.

- Head tilt and chin lift. Tilt the child's head a little backward with one hand. Don't tilt it too much, as this may actually make breathing more difficult. The fingers of the other hand should lift the chin so that it points relatively straight up. This is the "sniff" position.

OPEN THE AIRWAY
(Head tilt and chin lift)
▼
CHECK FOR BREATHING

▼	▼
Breathing	Not breathing
▼	▼
KEEP AIRWAY OPEN	**GIVE TWO BREATHS**
(Head tilt and chin lift)	(Check for chest movement)

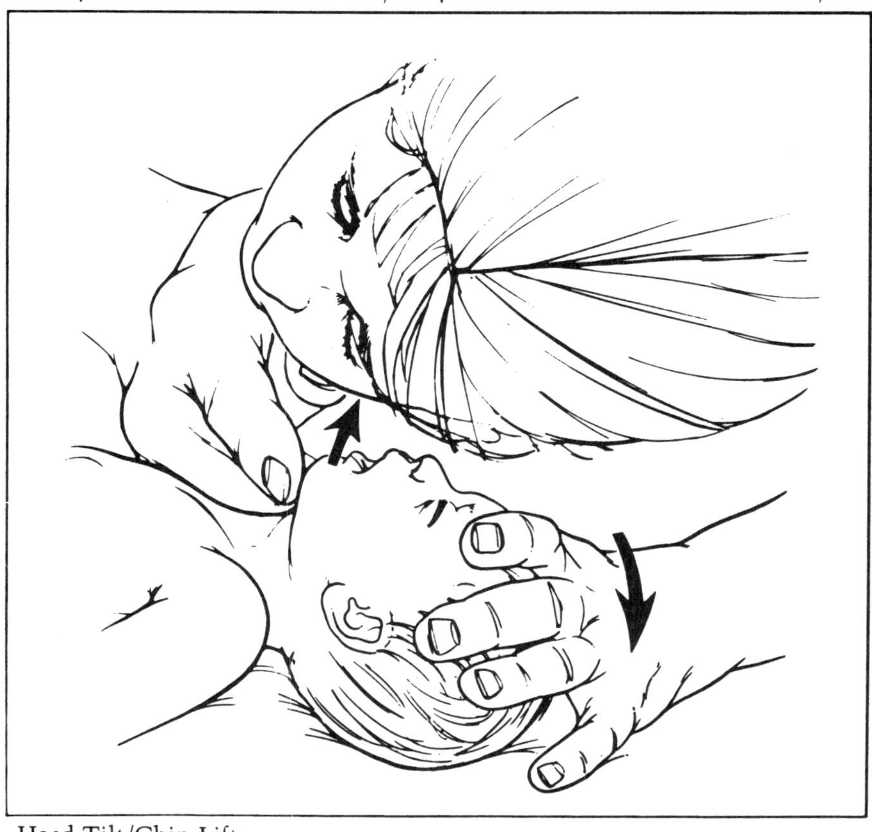

Head-Tilt/Chin-Lift

5. *Check for breathing* while maintaining an open airway
   LOOK for the chest or belly moving
   LISTEN for air moving
   FEEL for air moving from the nose or mouth

If the child is breathing and skin color is good, continue to maintain an open airway. Sometimes just opening the airway is enough to let your child breathe.

If the child is not breathing (or skin color is poor), proceed to breathe for the child with **RESCUE BREATHING:**

- ▼ **For an infant,** tightly seal your mouth over the infant's mouth and nose. Breathe once every three seconds or about 20 breaths per minute.
- ▼ **For a child**, pinch the child's nose tightly with the fingers of the hand that is maintaining the head tilt and make a mouth-to-mouth seal. Breathe once every four seconds or about 15 times a minute.

Two slow breaths (over two to three seconds) should be given initially. Breathe hard enough to make the child's chest move up and down. Do not breathe harder than necessary to make the chest move.

- ▼ **If air goes in**, continue rescue breathing and check for a pulse;
- ▼ **If no air goes in**, recheck the airway and, if open, consider the possibility of an obstruction and follow steps to relieve choking (see page 114).

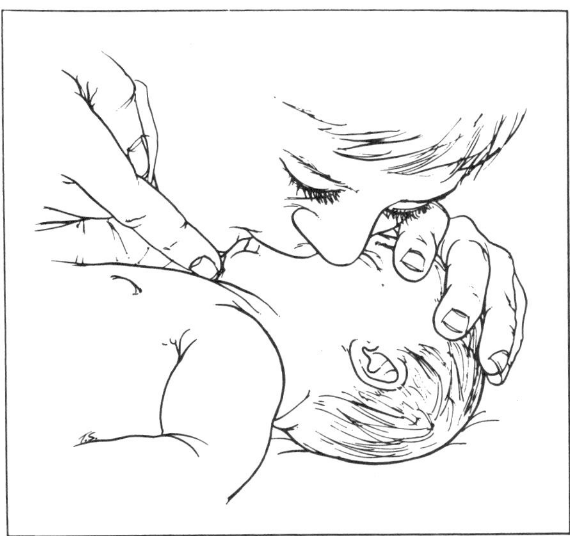

Mouth-to-mouth and nose seal.

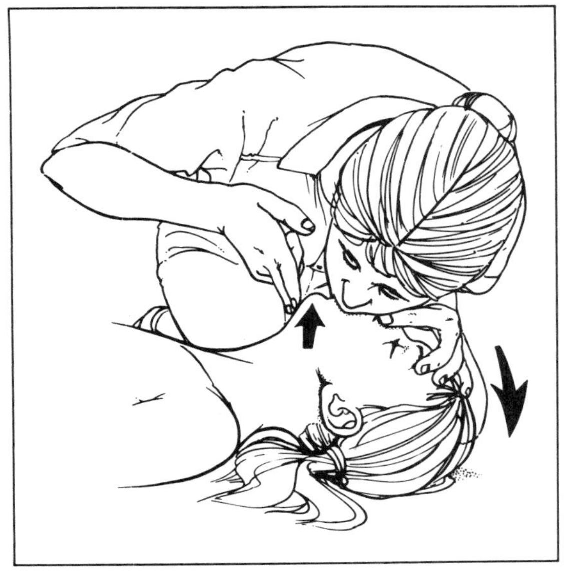

Mouth-to-mouth seal.

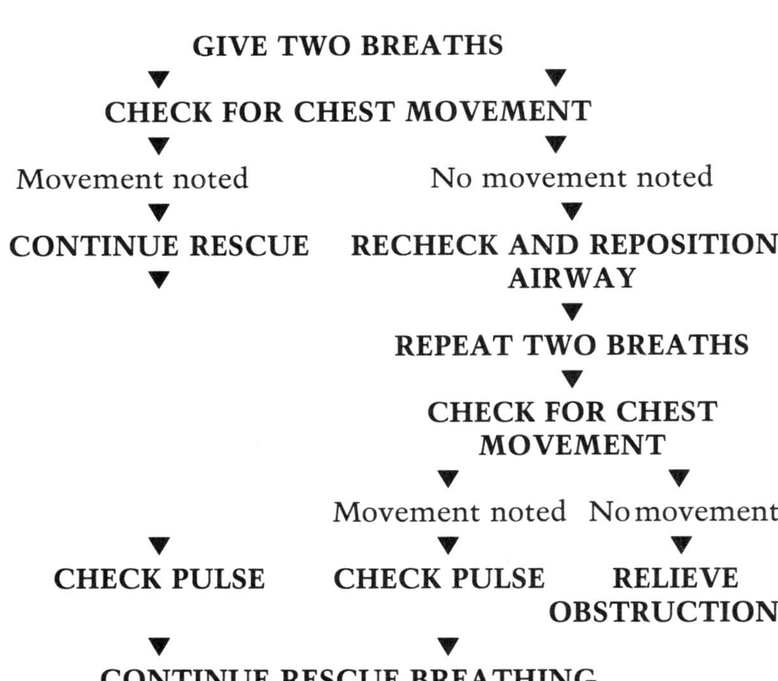
GIVE TWO BREATHS
CHECK FOR CHEST MOVEMENT
Movement noted
No movement noted
CONTINUE RESCUE
RECHECK AND REPOSITION AIRWAY
REPEAT TWO BREATHS
CHECK FOR CHEST MOVEMENT
Movement noted
No movement
CHECK PULSE
CHECK PULSE
RELIEVE OBSTRUCTION
CONTINUE RESCUE BREATHING

6. *Check pulse* to determine if there is a heartbeat, while maintaining an open airway and breathing for the child if necessary. Check the pulse at one of two sites:

▼ **Brachial pulse** is located on the inside of the upper armbetween the elbow and shoulder. It is useful in infants.

▼ **Carotid pulse** is useful in children over one year. It lies on the side of the neck between the windpipe and the strap muscles (major neck muscles).

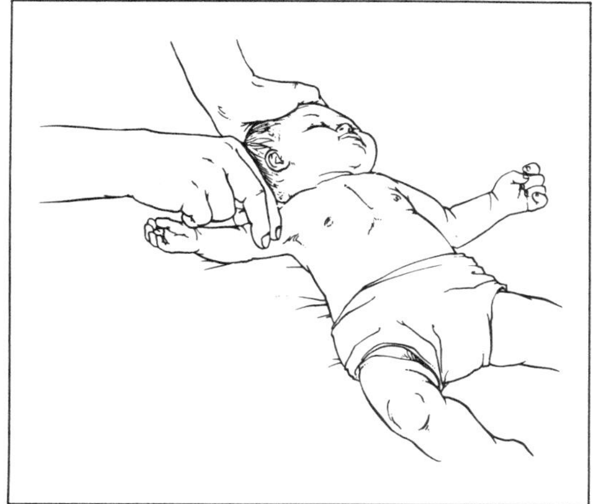

Locating and palpating brachial pulse.

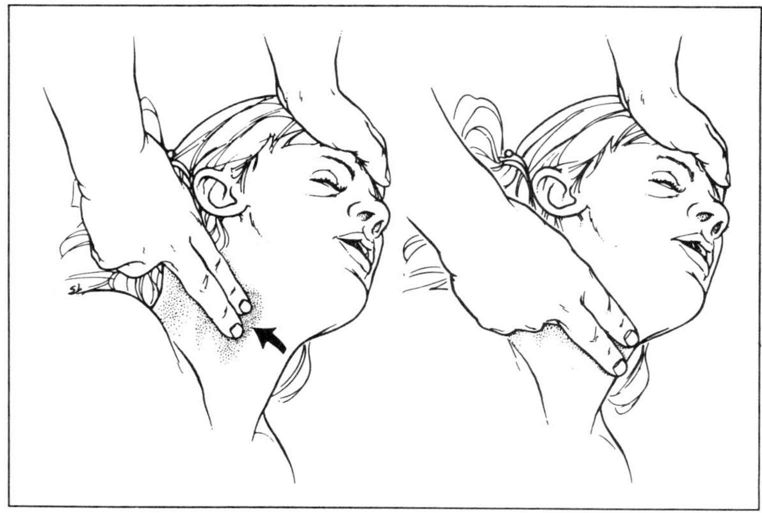

Locating and palpating carotid artery pulse.

▼ **If the child has a pulse** but is not breathing, continue rescue breathing;
▼ **If the child has no pulse** and is not breathing, continue rescue breathing and **BEGIN CHEST COMPRESSIONS**.

No pulse present	Pulse present
▼	▼
BEGIN CHEST COMPRESSIONS	**CONTINUE RESCUE BREATHING**

Compress breastbone 80 to 100 times per minute.
Give five chest compressions and then one breath;
Reassess every 10 cycles; continue.

7. *Performing chest compressions* allows you to pump blood around the body if the heart is not adequately doing this.

- Compressions must be accompanied by rescue breathing and should be done smoothly. The location for exerting the compression varies with the age of the child.

▼ **For an infant:**

Location: Position yourself at child's side. Draw an imaginary line between the nipples and place the index finger of your hand farthest from the baby's head on the breastbone beneath the imaginary line. The area for compressions is below the level of the index finger at the level of the middle and ring fingers. *Method:* Compress the breastbone using two fingers to a depth of one-half to one inch at a rate of 100 per minute (or five compressions per three seconds)

▼ **For a child (over one year):**

Location: Position yourself at child's side. Define the lower edge of the rib cage on the child's side with your middle and index fingers. Follow the edge to the notch where ribs and breastbone meet. Place your middle finger on the notch and your index finger next to the middle finger. Place the heel of your hand next to your index finger with the long axis parallel to the breastbone. *Method*: Compress the breastbone one to 1 1/2 inches at a rate of 80 to 100 times per minute.

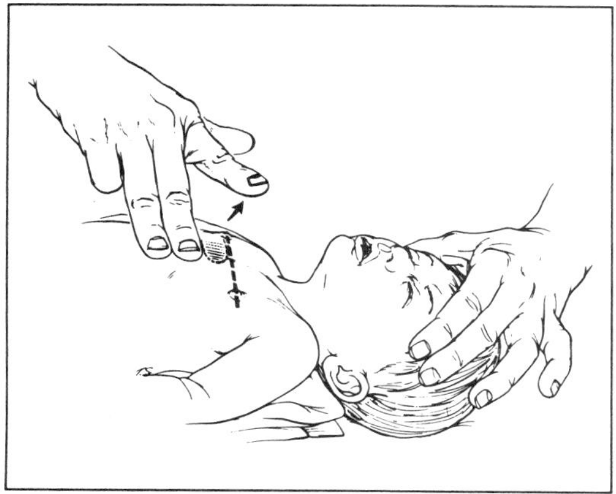

Locating finger position for chest compressions in infants.

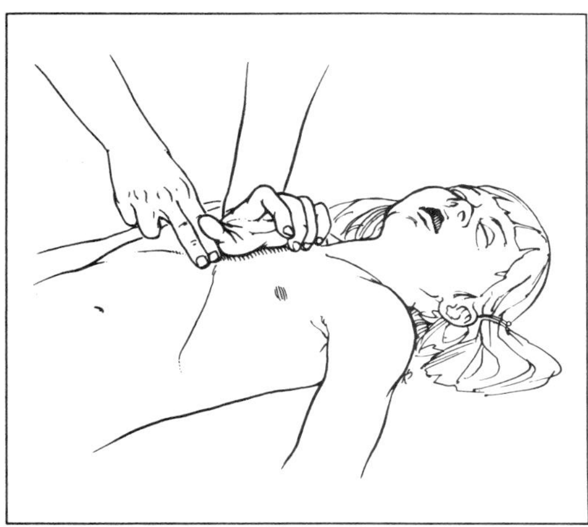

Locating hand position for chest compressions in child.

8. *Coordination of chest compressions and breathing* is essential. Give five chest compressions and then give one breath. Repeat the cycle 10 times and recheck your child. Call for help and continue CPR until your child arrives at a hospital for definitive care.

STEPS to RELIEVE CHOKING

Children may choke on, aspirate, or inhale small objects or foods such as peanuts or raisins. If your child has inhaled an object and is given two breaths with no air movement, immediate action is necessary.

- **For an infant:**
  Turn child over onto the belly, keeping the head lower than the trunk. Put the child on your thighs. Support the head. Give four quick back blows between the shoulder blades. If this is unsuccessful, turn the infant over and place him/her on your lap with the head lower than the trunk. Four chest thrusts are delivered in the same location used for external chest compression.
- **For a child:**
  Stand behind the child and wrap your arms around his/her waist with one hand made into a fist. The thumb side of the fist should rest against the belly in the midline slightly above the navel and below the breastbone. Six to 10 thrusts are delivered in rapid sequence. This is called the Heimlich maneuver.

If the child is lying down, position him/her face up and exert a thrust on the belly in the middle slightly above the navel and well below the breastbone. Again six, to 10 thrusts are given.

The child's mouth should be opened and if there is any foreign material, it should be removed if possible. Do not blindly poke around in the mouth.

GIVE FOUR BACK BLOWS

▼

GIVE FOUR CHEST THRUSTS

▼

CHECK MOUTH FOR FOREIGN OBJECTS

▼

RETRY RESCUE BREATHING

▼

CHECK FOR BREATHING

▼	▼
Movement noted	No movement noted
▼	▼
CONTINUE RESCUE BREATHING	**CONTINUE BACK BLOWS, BREATHING, CHEST THRUSTS, ETC.**
▼	
CHECK PULSE	

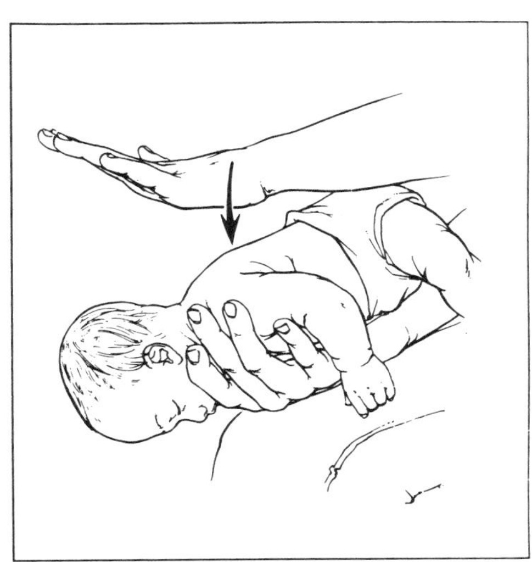

Back blow in infant.

Heimlich maneuver with child standing.

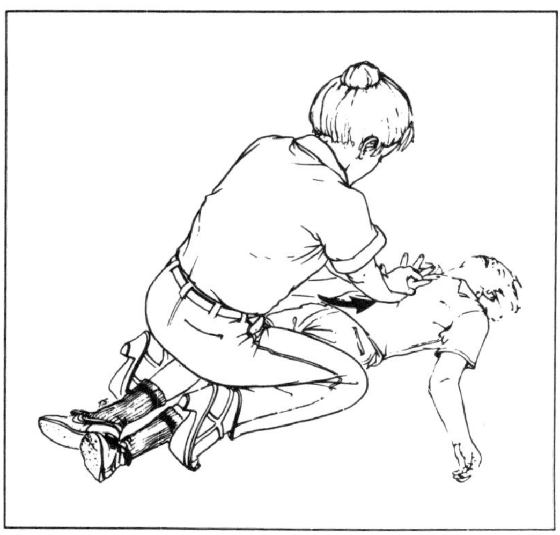

Heimlich maneuver with child lying.

Prevention of choking is particularly important since it is the second-greatest cause of home accidental deaths in children under four. Important steps to prevent choking include:

1. Do not allow young children to play with small objects. One suggestion is that children under three should not play with objects that are less than 1 1/4 inches in diameter or that fit into a circular cylinder 2 1/4 inches long;
2. Do not allow young children to put foreign objects or large pieces of food in their mouths;
3. Avoid peanuts, grapes and raisins.
4. Keep children quiet while eating. Running, walking and other activities can increase the risk of choking;
5. Keep your eye on balloons, as they can be inhaled when uninflated or after they burst;
6. Keep plastic bags, particularly those used for dry cleaning, away from your children, as they can be inhaled.

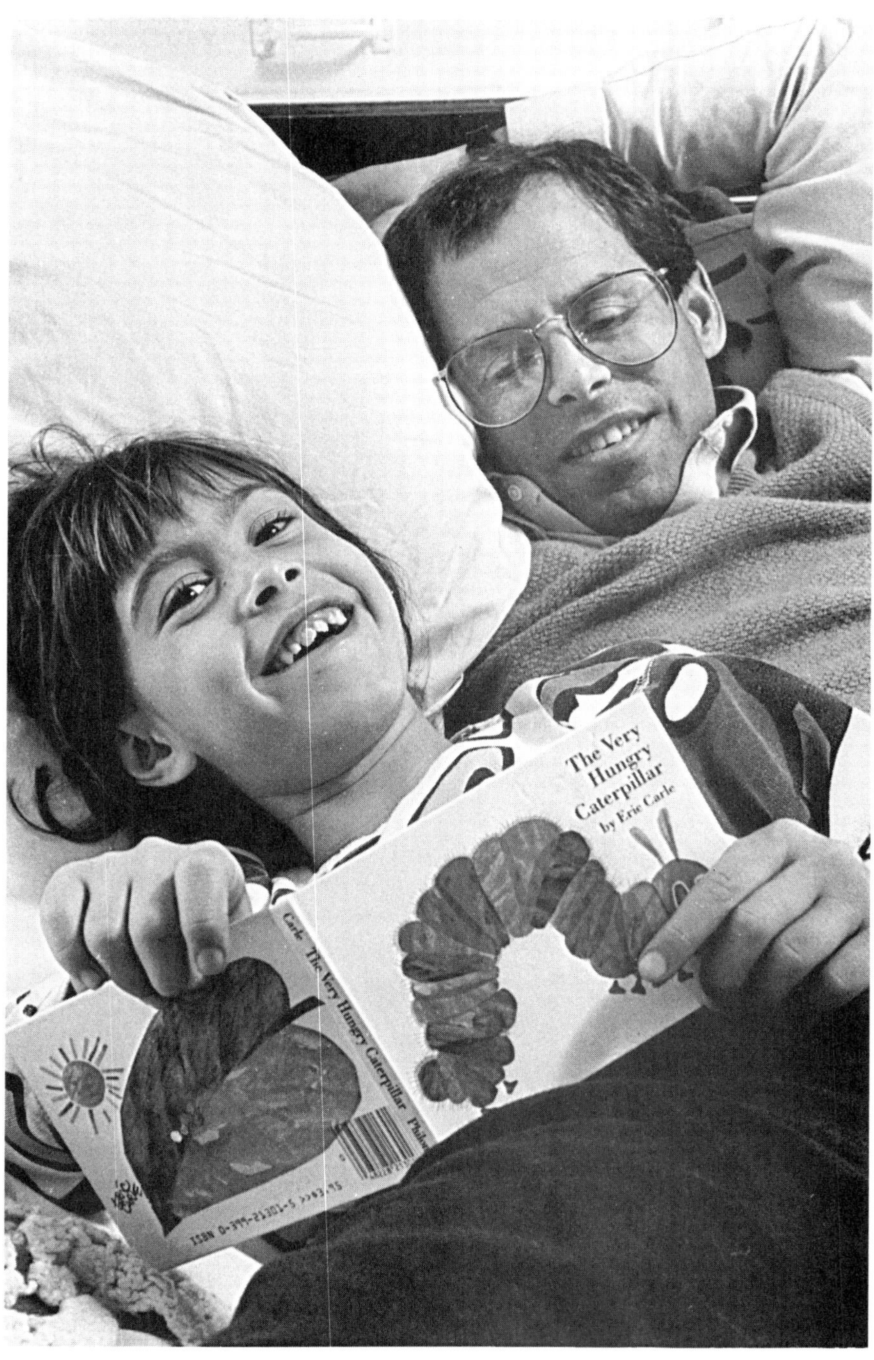
The Very
Hungry
Caterpillar
by Eric Carle
Carle The Very Hungry Caterpillar
ISBN 0-399-21301-5

SPECIFIC ILLNESSES and PROBLEMS

Chapter 8

ABDOMINAL PAIN

Sudden abdominal or belly pain often results from problems that may improve without medical attention. However, several problems can be potentially life threatening and require immediate action.

WHAT to LOOK for

Belly or abdominal pain can be described by its location, nature and associated problems.

Locate the pain. Different places are associated with specific problems. Although this is often difficult to do, finding out where the pain is may narrow down the problem. For instance, the liver is in the upper right part of the abdomen, the spleen in the upper left section, the stomach more central, and the kidneys in the lower part, often causing pain in the lower back.

The pain may be throughout the belly. This is common in gastroenteritis (stomach flu) with vomiting or diarrhea, as well as with abdominal muscle strain from an injury, hard coughing or constipation.

Describe the nature of the pain as steady, sharp, intermittent or crampy. Determine if the pain is getting worse, improving or remaining constant. Describe things that make the pain worse or better.

If the pain is associated with **vomiting** or **diarrhea**, determine the appearance, amount, and color of the material, as well as any presence of blood. Blood in the vomitus (red or "coffee grounds") implies that there is irritation or ulceration, while bloody stool (red or "black tarry") may result from a tear (fissure) of the rectum, allergy to soy or cow's milk, irritation of the lower bowel or damage to the intestines.

Appendicitis causes severe, sharp pain, beginning in the center of the belly and then moving to the lower right area. The belly is painful to touch, often hurting more on release after pushing in with your hand. In many children, particularly those under two years, it is difficult to make this diagnosis. A fever with vomiting, nausea and poor appetite is common.

WHEN to CALL YOUR CHILD'S DOCTOR

Call immediately if:

- Severe belly pain lasting over six hours;
- Severe pain with marked tenderness when the abdomen is touched, especially when the hand is released, that decreases when your child bends over or if your child is under one year of age;
- Moderate pain that is getting worse;
- Blood in vomitus or stool (digested blood looks black and tarry);
- Green (bile-stained) material in vomitus;
- Recent injury to belly;
- Change in mental alertness;
- Rapid or shallow breathing;

- Very sick appearance;
- Possible drug or poison ingestion.

Call within a few hours, usually following home treatment, if:

- Pain lasts over 24 hours or localizes to one part of the abdomen;
- Fever over 100° F (38.3° C) that lasts for 24 hours;
- Signs of dehydration (loss of water) including decreased urination, less moisture in diapers, dry mouth, no tears, weight loss, sleepiness or irritability;
- Jaundice (yellow skin or eyes);
- Painful, bloody or increased frequency of urination.

Call for an appointment if:

- Recurrent pain.

WHAT YOU CAN DO

If your child has none of the symptoms listed under "Call immediately," watch your child carefully for several hours. During this period, treat any vomiting or diarrhea with the usual, home approaches.

- Give small sips of clear liquids while allowing your child to rest;
- Treat fever with acetaminophen (see page 166). Avoid aspirin, laxatives and other medications not recommended by your doctor. Do not give pain medicines;
- Evaluate your child for changes every two hours. If your child does not improve, or worsens during a 12- to 24- hour period, call your doctor.

VISITING YOUR CHILD'S DOCTOR

A detailed history will be taken. A thorough evaluation of the abdomen and an examination of the rectum for tenderness and blood is common. Your doctor may consult with a surgeon.

Tests may include measures of infection (white blood-cell count), salt balance, hydration (amount of water), sugar, as well as an analysis of the urine and stool.

CAUTION

▼ Do not delay calling if there has been a rapid onset of severe abdominal pain;
▼ Bloody (or tarry) stools require evaluation immediately; watch for dehydration (loss of water);
▼ Watch the nature of the pain and the degree of sickness closely; contact your doctor again if either increases.

ANEMIA

Children with blood that has a low proportion of red blood cells (hematocrit) are anemic. The most common cause in children under two years of age is iron deficiency because of an inadequate diet. Loss of blood from bleeding or abnormal breakdown of blood (hemolysis) may also cause anemia.

WHAT to LOOK for

Mild anemia usually has no signs or symptoms. If severe, your child may be weak, tired, irritable and pale. Older children may behave differently or have learning or developmental problems. With very severe anemia, children are short of breath and have a rapid heart rate.

WHEN to CALL YOUR CHILD'S DOCTOR:

Call immediately if:
- Shortness of breath or rapid pulse.

Call within a few hours if:
- Unusual weakness, tiredness or irritability.

WHAT YOU CAN DO

- If there is an iron deficiency, change your child's diet to include more iron-rich foods such as meats, eggs, green vegetables and enriched cereals and breads. If your child is an infant, restrict milk intake to a maximum of 24 ounces per day.

• Initially, iron drops (Fer-in-Sol) should be taken as prescribed. Your child's blood will be rechecked in one to two weeks and again at one and two months to be certain that the anemia is improving. The stool may become black.

VISITING YOUR CHILD'S DOCTOR

After an initial dietary assessment, a physical examination may reveal evidence of anemia. If your doctor does not think the anemia is due to an unbalanced diet and low iron, potential sources of bleeding or blood breakdown will be explored.

A hematocrit or hemoglobin test provides a measure of the anemia. Evaluation of the red blood cells should confirm an iron deficiency. If the cause is uncertain, your doctor may consult a specialist in blood cells (hematologist).

CAUTION

▾ Change the diet to include iron-rich foods while giving extra iron if prescribed.

ASTHMA

Asthma is due to constriction and narrowing of the lower airway, often with inflammation and swelling of the airway. Allergies as well as infection or irritants in the air, such as dust or chemicals, may cause this. Wheezing often follows a respiratory infection or cold.

WHAT to LOOK for

Asthmatic children breathe with a rapid rate and wheezing (high-pitched sound in the chest, not rattling in the back of the throat). There may also be congestion, cough or fever. Some children may have only a prolonged cough.

In more serious cases, your child may develop difficult and rapid breathing, exaggerated movement of the chest and blueness of the lips and fingers (cyanosis). With worsening, your child may have difficulty speaking or becomes restless or sleepy. Complications may include lung infections with the sputum changing from white to yellow or green, or dehydration (loss of water) due to poor fluid intake.

Wheezing may be due to other problems such as pneumonia or the inhaling of fluid and foreign material into the lungs.

WHEN to CALL YOUR CHILD'S DOCTOR

Call immediately if:

- Breathing becomes more difficult or is not improving;
- Blue or dusky lips or nails;
- Difficulty speaking because of shortness of breath;
- Restlessness or excessive sleepiness.

Call within a few hours if:

- Breathing is getting worse, but there is no real distress;
- Signs of dehydration (loss of water) including decreased urination, less moisture in diapers, dry mouth, no tears, weight loss, sleepiness or irritability;
- Recent hospitalization for asthma;
- Steroids such as prednisone taken in the last year;
- Not improving after 24 hours of therapy;
- Persistent fever for the last 24 hours;
- Difficulty sleeping;
- Change of sputum from white to yellow or green;
- Medications not tolerated.

Call for an appointment if:

- There is a persistent cough;
- No resolution after two days.

WHAT YOU CAN DO

Keep your child calm by rocking, holding and being reassuring. Reduce activity and encourage warm fluids. Fluids are essential and often accepted in small sips; don't worry if your child doesn't take solids for a day or so. Keep track of whether your child is improving or getting worse. Make sure medications are taken, if prescribed.

You may have to give your child asthma medicines, commonly prescribed to be given every six hours (first dose is usually 1 1/2 times the regular dose). If the problem is caused by an infection or specific exposure such as dust, continue the medicine for at least 72 hours after the wheezing has ceased. If the problem is recurrent, your child may need prolonged medication, often using sustained-release forms, which require less frequent administration. The asthma medicines may cause vomiting or irritability, requiring a dosage change.

A special inhalation machine or pocket, hand-held inhaler may be used three to four times per day. This may be done in conjunction with other asthma medicines.

Ongoing therapy often requires a combination of asthma medicines, nebulizers (inhalation machines for medicine), avoidance of substances that trigger the attack, and occasionally, desensitization shots by an allergist. Be certain to remove bothersome items from the home.

If any adults in the household smoke, discuss the importance of not exposing your child to "passive smoking." Stop smoking.

VISITING YOUR CHILD'S DOCTOR

Your child's medical history will determine how severe past episodes have been, what factors (infection, irritants, stress) bring on attacks, and present medications. During the physical examination, blood pressure, heart and respiratory rates, and temperature will be measured, and your child's chest will be examined.

If your child is wheezing, your doctor may give oxygen and medicines either by a breathing treatment or shot to increase air movement (bronchodilators).

Your child's oxygenation may be measured. A blood sample from the artery may permit an accurate assessment of difficult breathing. If your child is on asthma medicines, a level is often measured. Children who respond poorly to the initial therapy may require a chest X-ray.

Hospitalization is indicated if your child is having marked problems breathing and is not getting better rapidly.

CAUTION

▼ Do not give more medication than prescribed. Asthma medications can cause side effects.

BITES—ANIMAL AND HUMAN

Children commonly experience animal bites; human bites occur while fighting.

WHAT to LOOK for

The bite will produce puncture wounds or damage to the skin or underlying tissue. Things to consider in deciding if a bite is serious include:

Location and depth of the wound

See if there is an injury to the deeper tissues or just a scrape. Bites to the hands, feet or face are serious, even if the wound looks minor.

Animal bites

Rabies may result from bites of skunks, foxes, coyotes, raccoons, wild dogs and cats, and bats. If a domestic dog or cat is sick or the attack was unprovoked, rabies should be considered. Rodents such as mice, rats, squirrels, hamsters, gophers, chipmunks, rabbits and hares do not normally carry rabies. If there is any question, the public health department can provide information about the local animal population.

Human bites

However innocuous or rare, children should be watched closely for infection.

Infection

Animal and human bites may become red, swollen, acutely tender or pus-filled. Children may develop a fever or become seriously ill and require immediate attention. When infection does occur, it usually does so within three days of the bite.

Children must have a current tetanus immunization (five years for a major injury and 10 years for a minor wound).

WHEN to CALL YOUR CHILD'S DOCTOR

Call immediately if:

- Biting animal can carry rabies (see above);
- Animal is sick or the bite was unprovoked;
- Bite is on the face, hands or feet;
- Bite produces a great deal of damage or bleeding or is deep.

Call within a few hours if:

- Wound may require sutures;
- Wound looks red, tender, swollen, drains pus or your child develops a fever;
- Tetanus immunization has lapsed;
- Prescribed medicines are not tolerated.

WHAT YOU CAN DO

- Thorough cleansing is probably the most important part of treatment. If there is bleeding, apply direct pressure on the wound; if not, wash the injury with soap and water for at least five minutes. Watch the bite closely for infection over the next three to five days;
- Update tetanus status;
- If the rabies status of the animal is unknown and rabies is a consideration, try to capture the animal and have the public health department observe it in isolation for 10 days;
- Most importantly, instruct your children not to play with unfamiliar animals or place their faces near dogs;
- Teach your children to play calmly and avoid frightening animals with loud sounds or unexpected, quick movements;
- Do not leave children unattended with dogs and other potentially dangerous animals.

VISITING YOUR CHILD'S DOCTOR

After determining the circumstances, your doctor will examine the extent and depth of the injury and the presence of infection, if any.

Your doctor will wash the wound thoroughly. Tetanus immunization will be checked and updated if necessary. If the wound is on the face, examination will determine the likelihood of leaving a bad scar. Sometimes, stitching will reduce the scar; however, sutures may increase the risk of infection. Despite this risk, sutures are often indicated in facial bites. Your doctor will also start antibiotics when bites involve the face or hands, cause extensive tissue damage or become infected.

If rabies is a risk, rabies vaccine can now be administered as a series of five injections given at the time of exposure and three, seven, 14 and 28 days later.

CAUTION

▼ Careful examination of the region of animal or human bites is necessary to determine if there is damage to deep tissues; look for infection.

BITES, INSECT

Insect bites usually cause only local reactions, but periodically, a reaction can cause difficulty breathing.

WHAT to LOOK for

Local pain, itching and hives (or welts) occur commonly and disappear over three to four hours. Insect bites may become infected.

Bites from poisonous spiders do occur. The bite of the black widow spider (shiny, black, button-shaped body with red hourglass markings on underside) produces immediate pain at the bite site followed by crampy abdominal pain, nausea, vomiting, headache or sweating. The bite of the brown recluse spider (one-half to one inch in length with violin-like markings on the back of the chest) causes pain at the site followed by formation of a blister. The blister may become dark with a great deal of tissue damage.

Severe reactions called *anaphylaxis* cause an asthma-like attack with the child rapidly developing wheezing and shortness of breath. This is extremely rare.

Tick bites are common, with the tick often imbedding itself in the scalp or at the back of the neck. Ticks may carry a number of diseases; removal usually eliminates any problems.

WHEN to CALL YOUR CHILD'S DOCTOR

Call immediately if:

- Evidence of shortness of breath, wheezing, rapid breathing or anaphylaxis (see above);
- Bite from a potentially poisonous spider (black widow or brown recluse);
- More than six bites by bees, wasps, hornets or yellow-jackets;
- Bad reaction to insect bites in the past.

Call within a few hours if:

- Pain, irritation or itching at the site of a bite beyond three to four hours;
- Fever or rash in the seven days following removal of a tick.

WHAT YOU CAN DO

Most children have minimal and rapidly disappearing reactions at the site of a bite. If a bee stinger is still present, you can usually remove it by scraping it off with your fingernail or using tweezers or a sterile needle. Pain and itching respond to cold packs placed on the site, often followed by a paste of baking soda. If itching is severe and prolonged, you can purchase an over-the-counter antihistamine, such as Benadryl, and give it to your child for 24 hours.

If ticks are present, remove them by covering the tick with alcohol, mineral oil, nail polish or an ointment. Pick up the tick's body with forceps and pull gently and steadily. Rarely, you may need to cut the tick off the skin.

If difficulty breathing or *anaphylaxis* occurs with this or previous episodes, purchase an emergency kit containing a prefilled syringe of epinephrine to keep at home and in the car for future use. A medical identification bracelet is also appropriate. Many physicians recommend desensitization.

Obviously, you cannot prevent insect bites, but you can teach your children to avoid going barefoot in places with many bees and spiders and to check themselves after hiking in tick-infested areas. You may want to use insect repellents.

VISITING YOUR CHILD'S DOCTOR

Your doctor will take a quick history. If wheezing or shortness of breath is present, your doctor will give medicine by injection or breathing treatment. In rare instances, fluids and drugs are injected by vein, and hospitalization is necessary. Your doctor will examine the site of the bite. If there is evidence of a bite from a poisonous spider, your doctor will take specific measures.

If a tick is still present, your doctor will remove it.

CAUTION

▾ Difficulty breathing following an insect bite is life threatening and requires immediate contact with your doctor.

BITES, SNAKE

Most snakes are not poisonous in the United States. Only 5 percent are poisonous including pit vipers, water moccasins, copperheads, rattlesnakes and coral snakes.

WHAT to LOOK for

Most snakebites cause reactions such as local swelling and redness at the site of the bite but no other injury.

Poisonous snakes usually have vertically elliptical, slit-like pupils; a facial pit between the eyes and nostril; a rattle and fangs. A bite can cause local swelling with red or purple areas, nausea, vomiting, sweats, chills and tingling of the tongue. This may progress rapidly.

WHEN to CALL YOUR CHILD'S DOCTOR

Call immediately if:

- Evidence or suspicion of a poisonous snakebite (local swelling and burning with red or purple areas is followed by nausea, vomiting, sweats, etc.).

Call within a few hours if:

- There is a severe local reaction to a nonpoisonous snakebite;
- Marked anxiety in your child occurs.

WHAT YOU CAN DO

Keep your child calm by holding and reassuring him/her.

If you suspect a poisonous snakebite, tie a broad, firm constrictive bandage (handkerchief, etc.) between the bite and the heart, at least two inches above the bite if on an arm or leg. Make it tight enough to cause the veins to stand out but do not allow the foot or hand to turn white. Loosen this tourniquet every 20 minutes for a few seconds.

Splint the arm or leg to reduce motion. Do not put the injured area in ice or cold water. If possible, keep your child's arm or leg lower than the rest of the body.

If possible, kill and identify the snake. Handle the head carefully, since it can deliver venom for as long as one hour after death.

Rapidly transport your child to a hospital.

VISITING YOUR CHILD'S DOCTOR

Your doctor will determine the nature of the bite and the suspected kind of snake. Often blood tests indicate any possible complications. If the snake is poisonous, your doctor will give antivenin and will usually hospitalize your child.

CAUTION

▼ Following a bite by a known or suspected poisonous snake, seek immediate attention.

BLOOD IN STOOL OR VOMITUS

Blood in the stool or vomitus is always abnormal and is usually due to gastrointestinal (stomach or gut) bleeding. Often, however, the "blood" is not significant. Something your child ate may cause the stool to appear red.

WHAT to LOOK for

Belly pain with bloody stools usually means there is some injury to the intestines. Your child may have crampy or continuous and severe pain. The stool usually has the appearance of "tar," i.e., tarry stools.

Diarrhea accompanies gastroenteritis or "stomach flu." There may be blood in the stool, but it is important to be sure that a child with severe pain does not have a more serious disease.

Mild bleeding, usually without pain, commonly results from tears (fissures) of the rectum. The blood is usually bright red and is on the surface of the stool rather than mixed within the stool. The child is often constipated. Allergy to cow or soy milk may cause mild bleeding. Swallowed blood can also appear as a positive test for blood in the stool.

Swallowed blood from a bloody nose or cut, an irritation of the stomach (gastritis), a stomach ulcer or prolonged violent vomiting may cause blood in the vomitus. Children with an irritation or ulcer usually have pain in the central, upper belly.

Eating iron and vitamins, red fruits and liquids, red meat, large numbers of chocolate sandwich cookies, bismuth, Pepto-Bismol, lead, licorice, charcoal, coal or red gelatin can make the stool or vomitus appear to have blood in it.

WHEN to CALL YOUR CHILD'S DOCTOR

Call immediately if:

- Large amount of blood in stool or vomitus;
- Blood in stool or vomitus accompanied by abdominal pain;
- Pale, weak or dizzy child.

Call within a few hours if:

- There is blood in stool or vomitus.

WHAT YOU CAN DO

Call your doctor. Try to recall foods that might have caused the change in stool or vomitus. Bring a specimen to your doctor.

Often, your doctor will find nothing serious going on and will attribute the blood in the stools to a rectal tear. Try to soften the stools by using prune juice, bran and roughage. Keep the rectal area dry. If your child has nothing worrisome, watch for problems over the next few days to be certain that there is no problem.

VISITING YOUR CHILD'S DOCTOR

Your doctor will try to exclude problems that require immediate attention and will perform a careful physical including a rectal examination.

Your child may need a number of tests, depending on the diagnosis. Blood tests will determine if your child is anemic, indicating a blood loss. Your doctor may take X-rays.

CAUTION

▾ Blood in the stool or vomitus, unless your child has obviously swallowed blood, requires immediate evaluation. The one exception is a tear at the rectum.

BLOODY NOSE

The blood vessels in the nose can bleed due to minimal injury or irritation, particularly in dry climates. A bloody nose is common after minimal injury from a cold or from nose picking.

WHAT to LOOK for

This occurs more commonly in winter in areas of low humidity. Occasionally, bleeding can occur from a foreign body in the nose, usually accompanied by an odor and drainage from the nostril. A bleeding problem can cause nosebleeds, but bleeding and bruising also occur elsewhere.

WHEN to CALL YOUR CHILD'S DOCTOR

Call within a few hours if:

- Continuing bleeding after constant and uninterrupted pressure for a minimum of two 10-minute periods for a total of 20 minutes.

Call for an appointment if:

- Recurrent nosebleeds;
- Accompanying bruises.

WHAT YOU CAN DO

Have your child blow his/her nose to remove clots. Then compress the soft and bony part of the nose downward toward the cheeks with thumb and forefinger for a minimum of 10 minutes. If this fails, hold the nose for an additional 10 minutes. Do not interrupt these periods to inspect the area. Keep your child calm by holding him/her on your lap, stroking the forehead and being reassuring. Optimally, have your child in a sitting position to minimize swallowing blood.

Reduce the frequency of future nosebleeds by placing petrolatum (Vaseline) or other ointment just inside the nostrils daily for four to five days. Use a cold-air vaporizer at night.

VISITING YOUR CHILD'S DOCTOR

Your doctor will have your child sit or lie down with his/her head back (depending on age and level of cooperation) and will perform compression of the nose, even if this has been done at home. Rarely is gauze packing or electric cautery necessary.

BURNS

Childhood burns can result from electrical contact, hot objects, hot water and other liquids, fires, chemicals and sunburn.

WHAT to LOOK for

Factors to consider in children with burns include the amount of skin burned, depth and location of the burn and how the burn occurred.

Amount of skin burned

The larger the area or body surface of the burn, the more severe. Your doctor should see your child if there are burns over 5 percent of the body. Children with burns over more than 10 percent of their body often require hospitalization.

Approximations may be inexact. In general, particularly in older children and adults, each arm is about 9 percent of the body surface, each leg 18 percent, the chest and back 18 percent each, and the head and neck 9 percent each.

Depth of the burn

First-degree burns have only reddening of the skin such as in sunburns;

Second-degree burns result in redness and fluid under the skin, forming blisters. They usually heal well but can produce complications such as fluid loss and infection;

Third-degree burns produce injury to the deep layers of the

skin. The skin has a hard, brownish surface, appearing charred. Often there is no feeling. These burns cause scarring and need specialized grafting.

Location

Burns involving the hands, face, eyes, ears, feet or genital area are particularly difficult to care for without specialized help.

Mechanism

How the burn occurred can influence the type of injury to be expected.

WHEN to CALL YOUR CHILD'S DOCTOR

Call immediately if:

- Second-degree burns cover more than 5 percent of the body surface;
- Any third-degree burns are present;
- Burns of the hands, face, eyes, ears, feet or genital area;
- Burns result from a fire in a closed space;
- Shortness of breath or rapid breathing;
- Burns result from an electrical source;
- Burns are caused from either acids or caustics;
- Explanation of how the burn occurred is suspicious (exclude child abuse);
- Other medical problems exist.

Call within a few hours if:

- Second-degree burns cover less than 5 percent of the body surface;
- First-degree burns cover more than 5 percent of the body surface;
- Increasingly painful burns, with tenderness, redness or draining pus develops;
- Tetanus immunization status is uncertain or needs updating.

WHAT YOU CAN DO

Remove clothing and apply cool water over the burn area using clean towels or cloths to reduce the amount of skin damage and pain. If the burn is totally first-degree, red and tender only, involves less than 10 percent of the surface area, this initial treatment is probably adequate.

Second-degree burns require more care. Blisters should be left intact. Remove the loose skin from broken blisters using clean tweezers—your doctor should handle this for large-area burns.

If the burn is a very small (1 to 4 percent) second-degree burn and does not require a doctor's visit, use an antibiotic ointment or cream or leave the wound open to the air. If prescribed by your doctor, use a special burn cream, Silvadene, and cover with a nonsticky dressing. Redress the burn in 24 hours and then every two to three days for a period of 10 to 14 days. If the bandage sticks, soak it in warm water before removing. While redressing, cleanse the surface with soap and water. Keep the dressing clean and dry. Elevate the extremity immediately to limit swelling and protect the area from further injury. Continue elevation for 24 to 48 hours or until you visit your child's doctor.

Treat tar burns by removing the tar with mineral oil and then treating as any other burn.

Electrical burns require evaluation by a doctor to determine the nature of the injury. Remove your child from the source, being careful to avoid electrical shock. If your child bites an electrical cord with a subsequent burn to the lip, your doctor should evaluate and watch the area closely.

Chemical burns initially require copious washing at the scene, usually before transport. Wash off or remove all contaminated clothing and rinse your child using a shower, hose or tub. Rinse eyes first if involved.

Prevention is the key to minimizing the frequency of burns.

Protect fireplaces, heating devices and hot objects, hide matches, discard flammable liquids, turn down water heaters to 120 degrees, and be alert to potential accidents. Install early smoke detection devices and fire extinguishers in high-risk areas. Develop an escape plan and conduct drills (Ch. 5).

VISITING YOUR CHILD'S DOCTOR

Your doctor will determine how the burn occurred and assess the extent and depth of the injury. If appropriate, your doctor will also examine your child for evidence of smoke inhalation or carbon monoxide poisoning. If the burn is extensive—greater than 10 percent of the body surface—or has significant third-degree involvement, your doctor will start an intravenous line to provide fluids. Your doctor will determine if your child needs a tetanus shot and will give pain medication if necessary. Hospitalization is often necessary for extensive burns or those in areas that are difficult to treat.

If the explanation of how the burn occurred does not make sense, your doctor will pursue the subject to make certain that the burn was accidental.

Burns due to electrical shocks usually require evaluation and often need hospitalization. Chemical burns from alkali or acid need copious washing.

CAUTION

- ▾ Second-degree burns over 5 percent of the body surface require evaluation, particularly if they include areas that are difficult to treat;
- ▾ Evidence of respiratory distress requires evaluation;
- ▾ Electrical and chemical burns require specific intervention.

CHEST PAIN

In contrast to adults, chest pain in young children is rarely due to serious heart disease.

WHAT to LOOK for

The nature of the pain and its relationship to other problems will help sort out the causes. Your child may have sharp or pressure-like pain accompanied by shortness of breath and rapid breathing, and perhaps fever, cough and systemic illness. A lung infection (pneumonia) can cause this. With trauma, the lung may rupture, and air will become trapped outside of the lung (pneumothorax). A pneumothorax can occur spontaneously.

Chest pain occurs with movement. If due to muscle spasm, pressing on the site of discomfort will reproduce the pain. This usually follows heavy lifting or exercising. An irritation of the lung lining (pleurisy) relates to a transient sensation of "catching" at the end of a big breath and usually disappears after the deep breath.

Children, particularly adolescents, may breathe fast or *hyperventilate* when stressed or excited. This may cause chest pain which resolves rapidly when the breathing slows down. The lips and hands are usually numb and tingling. Anxiety can often precipitate chest pain, commonly following a recent heart attack in a family member or friend.

WHEN to CALL YOUR CHILD'S DOCTOR

Call immediately if:

- Severe chest pain;
- Shortness of breath or rapid breathing;
- Irregular or rapid pulse;
- Wheezing or history of asthma;
- Trauma preceding the onset of pain;
- If you suspect underlying cardiac disease.

Call within a few hours if:

- Fever, cough or other symptoms of an infection;
- Anxiety or hyperventilation;
- Moderate pain lasting over two hours.

Call for an appointment if:

- Recurrent pain.

WHAT YOU CAN DO

Determine if there is rapid breathing, shortness of breath or marked indentation of the chest or abdomen with each breath. These symptoms require evaluation by a physician. Children with pneumonia or asthma may have chest pain and require specific medications. Rarely, chest pain caused by severe coughing may require suppression of the cough, particularly if it is interfering with sleep.

Most commonly, chest pain is due to an injury of the chest wall that results in muscle spasm. Aspirin, heat packs and rest should partially relieve the discomfort. If severe, your child may need medication for pain and muscle relaxation.

Children or adolescents who breath too fast (hyperventilation) respond to breathing into a paper bag or cupped hands held loosely over the nose and mouth until breathing slows down. Your reassurance is particularly important.

VISITING YOUR CHILD'S DOCTOR

Your child's history helps to focus on the cause of the pain. Your doctor will exclude lung and heart disease and preceding trauma and will assess sources of stress and anxiety. The physical examination will help confirm the clinical impression.

Many children will need a chest X-ray to look for pneumonia or pneumothorax. Rarely, your child will require a heart tracing (EKG) or other test.

CAUTION

▼ Severe chest pain with associated respiratory distress should receive immediate attention.

COLD OR UPPER RESPIRATORY INFECTION (URI)

Colds are common in children, increasing in number as your children come in contact with others, particularly in day-care settings. Preschoolers can have up to five to eight colds per year. Viruses cause colds.

WHAT to LOOK for

Your child may have congestion with a runny or stuffy nose, often with a sore throat, posterior nasal drip, cough, headache, red eyes, hoarseness or fever. He/she may have a poor appetite and be sleepy and irritable. Muscles are often tender and may ache. Occasionally, colds lead to complications such as ear infections or pneumonia.

WHEN to CALL YOUR CHILD'S DOCTOR

Call immediately if:
- Difficult or rapid breathing;
- Marked irritability or listlessness.

Call within a few hours if:
- Ear pain;
- Chest pain;
- Sore throat with or without white spots on tonsils;
- No improvement or persistent fever after 72 hours;
- Infant is under three months of age;
- Skin under the nose becomes raw or cracked, often with golden crusting;
- Discharge from the nose becomes green and contains pus.

WHAT YOU CAN DO

Colds require little therapy. To make your child more comfortable, take the following steps. In the younger child, use water nosedrops to reduce congestion; then clean the nose with a bulb syringe (usually given to parents when their child is born). In the older child, decongestants and antihistamines, such as Actifed, Rondec or Dimetapp may offer relief, particularly if the problem is a runny nose. A cold-air vaporizer may reduce the symptoms.

Fever medicine such as acetaminophen (Tylenol, Tempra, etc.) should be used to keep the temperature relatively normal (see page 166). Antibiotics are not needed.

Encourage and push fluids. It is not crucial that your child eat any solids for a day or two until the cold resolves somewhat; fluids are essential!

VISITING YOUR CHILD'S DOCTOR

The visit will include a history and physical examination. Your doctor will discuss specific problems and begin fever medicines and decongestants.

COLIC

Prolonged periods of fussiness occurring repeatedly over several days are noted in up to 10 percent of children, usually between two weeks and three months of life. This is normal. Little is known about this condition, but it is thought to be caused by gas-like abdominal pains. Many people think it occurs in children who are particularly sensitive to stimuli. It is a benign condition that resolves spontaneously when babies get older.

WHAT to LOOK for

Children cry and are irritable at a similar time of each day, the evening being most common. Babies are difficult to console and may have their legs drawn up. A number of steps are useful but may not always calm the child. In between episodes, babies are consolable.

Other causes of irritability can include dirty diapers, hunger, illness, diaper pin(s) sticking the child, teething, drug poisoning and unrecognized injuries or illness.

WHEN to CALL YOUR CHILD'S DOCTOR

Call within a few hours if:

- Vomiting or diarrhea;
- Crying that lasts over four hours;
- Fever, runny nose, cough or vomiting;
- Baby is younger than two weeks or older than four months;
- Parents are tired and getting increasingly frustrated.

WHAT YOU CAN DO

First, make sure that there is no specific cause for crying (e.g., pin in clothing or thread around digit). Then, use any number of activities to console the baby. Rhythmic activities such as rocking, automatic swings, rides or walking are often helpful. Try cuddling your child, wrapping him/her in a Snugli, playing soothing music or giving him/her a pacifier for sucking. Each child responds uniquely. It is important to discover those things that are useful for your particular infant.

On occasion, you must allow your child to just cry him/herself to sleep. Make sure that your child is not hungry (i.e., has eaten in the last 2 to 2 1/2 hours), that the nipple was not plugged and that the diaper is not dirty. You may have difficulty listening to your child crying, but responding every time gets tiresome very quickly and encourages your child to be increasingly demanding. All children prefer being held, rocked or fed constantly, and crying is often an attempt to get this. Setting some limits and making the decision to not respond every time your baby cries will discourage increasingly demanding behavior. This is important for parents and for children! Reach a reasonable balance and discuss it with your doctor. Talk with others about your frustrations. Remember who is supposed to be in control!

VISITING YOUR CHILD'S DOCTOR

Rarely does your child need to visit the doctor for colic. However, if you note anything worrisome or the incidents are prolonged,you may want to take your child in for a careful history and physical exam. Your doctor may give some helpful hints that may console your child and reassure you. It is imperative that parents be honest in talking about their frustrations.

CONSTIPATION

Children have many patterns of bowel movements. They *normally* have infrequent movements, sometimes going once every three to four days. Children may develop problems when there is pain or discomfort with bowel movements. Dietary changes can cause constipation. A change in bowel pattern, rather than the number of days between movements, is of greatest importance.

WHAT to LOOK for

Pain or discomfort with bowel movements can occur with hard stools or, more frequently, when there is a tear (fissure) in the rectum. The stool may have bright-red blood streaks. Rarely, patients with severe diaper rash will withhold bowel movements due to pain.

Beyond the infant period, constipation may occur when toilet training begins and parents are giving a great deal of attention to bowel movements. Your child may retain stool, often for so long that he/she develops crampy abdominal (belly) pain, usually decreasing temporarily after stooling (see page 81).

In older children, stool retention may recur due to emotional factors and stress. These children often have abdominal pain, again decreasing partially with movements.

If retention occurs over a long enough period, liquid stools may develop around the hardened mass and leak out.

WHEN to CALL YOUR CHILD'S DOCTOR

Call within a few hours if:

- Painful bowel movements;
- Blood in stool;
- No stool for five days;
- Abdominal pain for more than two hours.

Call for an appointment, usually after beginning home treatment, if:

- Recurrent abdominal pain;
- Soiling;
- Tear or fissure around rectum;
- Medications contributing to problem;
- Associated with toilet training.

WHAT YOU CAN DO

Changing the diet is usually sufficient. For your baby, give one tablespoon of Karo syrup (light or dark) in every four to eight ounces of formula, milk or water. Encourage foods like prune juice and strained apricots, peaches, pears, prunes and other fruits when appropriate.

Be supportive, particularly if the problem is related to toilet training. Slow down and let your child do it at his/her own pace.

Encourage older children to drink prune juice and to eat bran products. Push fruits and vegetables and other sources of fiber and roughage such as celery, oranges, bran flakes, prunes, figs, dates, peaches, and pears. Fluid intake is essential. Discourage milk products, bananas and applesauce, since they are constipating.

On rare occasions, use natural laxatives, such as Maltsupex or Metamucil, usually starting with a dose of one-half to one tablespoon twice a day and increasing as necessary.

Treat rectal tears by softening the stool and keeping the area dry. Apply a cream after diaper changes to soothe.

Do not use enemas and suppositories; they may be dangerous.

VISITING YOUR CHILD'S DOCTOR

If your home treatment is not successful, your doctor will want to make sure no medical problems exist. After ruling out any problems, your doctor may have other suggestions, usually involving a more aggressive approach to dietary changes.

Children who are soiling usually require an intense program of both medical and emotional support. This may involve a combination of laxatives, lubricants and stool softeners. You and your doctor should do an in-depth evaluation of contributing emotional factors.

CONVULSIONS OR SEIZURES

A seizure (convulsion) is a transient disturbance of brain function, usually caused by an area of irritation in the brain. There are many forms of convulsions and many causes. For children who have had convulsions in the past, the most common cause for a recurrence is forgetting to take a few doses of anti-seizure medicines.

The vast majority of seizures are known as *febrile seizures* and occur in 2-5 percent of *normal* children as a result of a high fever. They usually stop by themselves and do not cause any long-term problems.

WHAT to LOOK for

Convulsions commonly cause a jerking movement of the extremities, with associated rolling of the eyes, and loss of control of urine and stool. One side of the body may be more affected than the other. Children are not usually responsive or aware of what is going on during the convulsion. Breathing difficulty may occur. Although most convulsions are self-limited and last only 60 to 90 seconds, episodes may go on for some time until medicines are given and the seizures are stopped. Following a convulsion, children are usually sleepy and rest for a period.

Find out if your child has had a fever or been sick, has experienced recent head injury, or has possibly taken any drugs. Ascertain if there is a history of past convulsions either in the child or in members of the immediate family. If anti-seizure medications are normally taken, it is important to determine if all doses are being taken.

A child having a *febrile seizure* usually also has a fever, most commonly caused by a cold or ear infection. The convulsions usually involve all extremities, and stop without therapy within 15 minutes. The seizure is often the first time you realize that your child is sick.

Rarely, children with seizures have episodes of staring or unusual movement of the face, tongue or mouth.

WHEN to CALL YOUR CHILD'S DOCTOR

Call immediately (call 911) if:

- Child's first seizure;
- Convulsion still going on;
- Difficulty breathing;
- Blue color of skin, lips, fingernails;
- Child has fever;
- Child not awake and alert.

Call within a few hours if:

- Any seizure, if stopped spontaneously;
- Child having trouble taking anti-seizure medications;
- Episode of staring or unusual movement of the face, tongue or mouth;
- Child had a febrile seizure, was evaluated and now has a prolonged temperature (for more than 36 hours) or is exhibiting behavioral changes, vomiting, headache, stiff neck or nonblanching rash.

WHAT YOU CAN DO

First, make sure that your child can breathe as easily as possible by putting his/her head in the "sniff" position to open the airway as much as possible. If your child is having great trouble breathing or has stopped breathing, start using the rescue breathing techniques described earlier (see page 106).

Try to make sure that your child doesn't hurt him/herself by striking his/her arm, leg or head. If your child's mouth is open, insert something soft like a washcloth to prevent the teeth from clenching tightly.

Arrange for rapid transport of your child to the hospital for treatment of the convulsions and evaluation of their cause, unless there is a history of recurrences.

If your child has a fever and is slowly waking up from the convulsion, begin medicines to bring the fever down.

VISITING YOUR CHILD'S DOCTOR

The first priority is to give oxygen and to make sure that your child is breathing normally. Your doctor will then attempt to stop the seizures, if they are ongoing, by using any one of a number of medications.

Attention will then turn to prevention of recurrences and assessment to determine the cause of the seizures. This will involve a number of blood, X-ray and other tests, depending on the various causes that are being considered.

If your child had a febrile seizure, your doctor will review with you that this type is usually harmless and occurs in 2 to 5 percent of normal children. There is only a very slightly increased risk of developing seizures later on. Rarely are there any long-term problems. Anti-seizure medications are rarely used. The visit to your doctor will focus on bringing down your child's temperature using Tylenol, Tempra, etc., and determining what infection your child has that caused the high fever. Common infections, as well as serious infections of the nervous system, will be considered.

CAUTION

▾ Make sure your child's airway is open and breathing is adequate;
▾ Your doctor should see your child to determine the cause of the seizure, even if it has stopped.

COUGH

An irritation of the airway or lungs causes coughing, which serves as a protective reflex to prevent mucus or pus from accumulating.

WHAT to LOOK for

A runny nose, sore throat and fever often accompany a cough. Allergy or irritation of the posterior throat may cause a dry, hacking, tickling cough. A posterior nasal drip tends to cause coughs that are worse at night when your child is lying down.

Coughing is sometimes a sign of lung problems. If accompanied by rapid breathing, coughing can mean there is pneumonia, particularly if your child has a fever. Children with asthma may have a cough, and it may be the only symptom that parents notice.

Young children may inhale small objects such as toys, peanuts and raisins without being noticed by parents. This can produce immediate problems or may result in only a chronic cough and some minimal wheezing.

Croup has a unique cough that sounds like a "barking seal." Your child may have *stridor* (a harsh sound when he/she breathes), exaggerated chest movement and distress (see page 151).

WHEN to CALL YOUR CHILD'S DOCTOR

Call immediately if:

- Shortness of breath, rapid breathing rate or difficulty breathing;
- Blueness of lips or nails;
- Breathing stopped, even momentarily;
- Spasms that cause choking, passing out, a bluish color of lips or persistent vomiting;
- Blood in sputum or mucus;
- Sudden onset of violent coughing in a child who might have inhaled a small object. Any other suggestion of foreign-body inhalation.

Call within a few hours if:

- Wheezing;
- Croupy, "barking-seal" type cough with any difficulty breathing;
- Minimal increase in breathing rate;
- Fever for more than 72 hours;
- Your child is younger than three months;
- Cough produces yellow-green material;
- Chest pain.
- Vomiting occuring repeatedly with coughing.

Call for an appointment if:

- Cough lasting more than two weeks;

- Cough interfering with sleep.

WHAT YOU CAN DO

Treatment depends on the type and cause of the cough. Children over four years can suck on cough drops or hard candy. You can make a good soothing mixture at home by mixing equal amounts of honey (corn syrup for children under one year) and lemon concentrate. Also use warm liquids such as tea.

Cough syrups are rarely useful, although some expectorants may loosen secretions. Very rarely, when the cough is interfering with sleep, work or school, or causing vomiting or chest pain, your doctor may prescribe a stronger cough medicine containing dextromethorphan (DM) or codeine. Use these with caution because they reduce the protection that coughing gives the lungs. They will not eliminate coughing entirely.

Coughs due to posterior nasal drip worsen at night. Give decongestants before bedtime; use a cold-air vaporizer in your child's bedroom.

Encourage fluid intake. Minimize or eliminate smoking from the house.

VISITING YOUR CHILD'S DOCTOR

The examination will focus on the lungs as well as the ears, nose and throat. If your doctor suspects a lung infection or the inhalation of a foreign body, your child will usually have a chest X-ray. Only if there is evidence of pneumonia or infection elsewhere will your doctor prescribe antibiotics.

CAUTION

▾ Coughing is only a symptom. Prolonged coughing, coughing associated with a high fever or coughing possibly following aspiration of a foreign body indicate the need for your doctor's evaluation.

CROUP

Inflammation of the airway at the voice box causes difficulty breathing. It is usually due to a virus.

WHAT to LOOK for

Children with croup are usually under three years and develop a cough that sounds like a "barking seal" preceded by a runny nose, cough, hoarseness and fever. Croup generally gets worse in the middle of the night between 2:00 and 6:00 a.m. with a crowing sound while breathing. Most children emit this crowing sound only when upset or anxious. The difficulty may quickly worsen to the extent that the child is gasping for air, with marked accentuation of chest movement. Croup usually resolves over a period of three to four days.

More worrisome is the child who rapidly develops a crowing sound when breathing in and out while at rest. This child may appear very sick, with a high fever, difficulty handling secretions, drooling and a preference for sitting up. These symptoms are due to inflammation of the epiglottis, which sits above the windpipe and can block the air passage. In contrast to croup, epiglottitis is due to a specific bacteria known as *H.influenzae* and may progress very rapidly. Rarely, children inhaling a foreign body may have a similar reaction.

WHEN to CALL YOUR CHILD'S DOCTOR

Call immediately if:

- Crowing constantly at rest or when upset;
- Shortness of breath, difficulty breathing or rapid respiratory rate;
- Increasing agitation or sleepiness;
- Blueness of lips or nails;
- Difficulty handling secretions or drooling;
- High fever in toxic child;
- Preference for sitting up with the chin protruding forward;
- Potential inhalation of foreign body.

Call within a few hours if:

- Crowing when child is very upset and crying;
- Evidence of dehydration noted by decreased amount of urination, fewer wet diapers, listlessness irritability, or dry mucous membranes.

WHAT YOU CAN DO

Give mist continuously. Use a vaporizer (cold preferred to reduce the risk of burns) in your child's bedroom. Use two, if needed, to generate enough mist. While this is being set up or if your child gets worse, take your child to the bathroom, close the door, run hot water to generate steam and sit or stand, soothing your child, as the steam fills the room. Do not put the child in the scalding water. If there is increasing discomfort, taking your child outside into the cold air may reduce the distress.

Keep your child calm by holding, rocking, reading and being soothing, while pushing fluids, often in small sips. Do not worry if your child will not take solids for a day or so; drinking is more important.

It is imperative to watch your child closely, paying particular attention to worsening breathing. This is one of the few circumstances when sleeping in your child's room may be reassuring.

VISITING YOUR CHILD'S DOCTOR

Your doctor will evaluate the amount of breathing difficulty by determining the presence of crowing while resting or crying, the rate of breathing and the amount of accentuation of breathing movements. If there are problems at rest, your doctor will usually hospitalize your child. Your doctor may give two medications: one administered by a breathing treatment and steroids given as a shot or liquid

If your child appears extremely ill (toxic) and there is potential infection of the epiglottis, your doctor will look at your child's throat in the hospital, often in the operating room under controlled conditions.

CAUTION

▾ When a crowing sound is present at rest, your doctor should evaluate your child. Hospitalization is usually necessary.

DIARRHEA

Frequent liquid or soft stools may be normal or may represent a change due to irritation or infection of the intestines. Allergy or too many antibiotics (especially amoxicillin or ampicillin) may also contribute.

Breast-feeding often causes yellow, mushy stools up to 12 times per day after feedings; a sudden change in pattern may indicate an abnormality.

WHAT to LOOK for

Infants with diarrhea have liquid, runny stools, often with enough water loss to produce a water ring around the solid material. Older children with diarrhea commonly have several runny stools per day.

Viral gastroenteritis (stomach flu) is common with children and is accompanied by fever, runny nose and sore throat. Vomiting is frequent. Diarrhea caused by other factors can make children very sick, with marked abdominal (belly) cramping and pain, fatigue, and nausea. Illness can follow eating contaminated food.

The stool may contain mucus or blood.

In children with a great deal of water loss due to vomiting or diarrhea, dehydration (loss of water) may develop, particularly in those who are reluctant to take fluids.

WHEN to CALL YOUR CHILD'S DOCTOR

Call immediately if:

- Blood in stool;
- Severe belly cramps or vomiting for more than two hours;
- Increasing frequency of stools or water loss;
- Evidence of dehydration (loss of water) including decreased

urination, less moisture in diapers, dry mouth, no tears, rapid breathing, weight loss, sleepiness or irritability;
- High fever or sick and toxic looking;
- Vomiting clear liquids.

Call within a few hours if:
- Diarrhea increases in frequency or amount with more than 10 episodes of vomiting or diarrhea in 24 hours;
- Diarrhea not improving after 24 hours of taking clear liquids, or not completely gone after three to four days;
- Mucus in stool;
- Fever for more than two days (call immediately if your child is less than three months old and has a fever);
- Child is taking medication.

Call for appointment if:
- Mild diarrhea has occurred for one week or more.

WHAT YOU CAN DO

Reduce or eliminate all solids from the diet; offer clear fluids. Children can easily go several days without solids.

Push, encourage and force liquids to make sure that too much water is not lost. Do this in a kind and supportive manner in very small amounts, particularly if there has been any vomiting. In the young child with vomiting and diarrhea, many people actually give a teaspoon of liquid at a time until the vomiting has at least partially resolved.

Specific products that are ideal for infants include Lytren and Pedialyte. Products available at home include Gatorade, soda (de-fizzed at room temperature) and liquid Jell-O (one package mixed with a quart of water instead of a pint). If the diarrhea is mild, it is often adequate to make your child's formula half-strength by adding twice as much water; in the breast-fed child, give a little supplemental water.

After a prolonged course of diarrhea, younger children should avoid milk products for one to two weeks, soy formulas (Isomil, ProSoBee or Soyalac) are good substitutes. If on milk, merely reduce the intake of such products while substituting other fluids. Do not use boiled skim milk. Kool-Aid and similar products are not good for diarrhea because they contain few salts.

In older children, push clear liquids. Defizzed, room temperature soda is acceptable, and your child may accept it enthusiastically.

When you see some improvement on this liquid diet, introduce other foods slowly. Reintroduce infants over six months to applesauce, strained bananas and carrots. Give crackers and dry toast to older children. As tolerated, start other items in your child's normal diet over the next three to four days, avoiding bran and raw fruits and vegetables.

Stop medications causing diarrhea (ampicillin or amoxicillin); call your doctor for alternatives. Drugs such as Kaopectate have no value, and, in fact, drugs such as Lomotil can cause real problems in children. Antibiotics are rarely useful.

VISITING YOUR CHILD'S DOCTOR

Your doctor will first make sure that your child is not dehydrated. If there is evidence of problems, your doctor will want to push fluids by mouth or intravenously; hospitalization may be required. A careful history often points to likely causes of the problem.

An examination of the stool may determine the cause of the diarrhea while an analysis of the urine assesses hydration. Additional studies may be necessary if the diarrhea is an ongoing source of concern.

The plan for therapy will require careful review.

CAUTION

▾ Do not use skim milk. Do not use anti-diarrheal medications;

▾ Push clear liquids while watching for evidence of dehydration.

EAR PAIN OR INFECTION

Ear pain is common in children and is usually caused by infection of the ear canal or the middle ear, with accumulation of fluid under pressure. Congestion blocks the normal drainage of the middle ear through the eustachian tube, allowing fluid to build up.

WHAT to LOOK for

Your child may have ear pain on one or both sides. Runny nose, sore throat, fever, irritability and increased crying are often present. Changing behavior or irritability are responses to pain. Ear pain may be only one part of a more serious infection.

If ear infections continue untreated, the eardrum may drain pus. Rarely, children with recurrent problems will develop a hearing loss.

When there is a rapid change in altitude such as descending in an airplane or driving down a mountain, ear pain may develop. This usually gets better with swallowing or holding the nose closed while blowing.

Pain in the ear when moved or touched does not always mean the middle ear is infected. Infection or irritation of the ear canal can occur from swimmer's ear or from drainage of the middle ear through a hole in the eardrum.

WHEN to CALL YOUR CHILD'S DOCTOR

Call immediately if:

- If your child exhibits marked irritability, sleepiness, stiff neck or looks sicker than expected;
- High temperature over 103°F (39.9° C);
- Severe pain, causing child to scream.

Call within a few hours if:

- Temperature over 101°F (38.3° C) for 12 hours;
- Ear pain for over one hour or tugging, rubbing or pulling ear;
- Drainage from ear;

- Pain with movement or when touching ear;
- After starting treatment, no improvement after 36 hours or fever present after 72 hours.

Call for an appointment if:

- There is any question of decreased hearing.

WHAT YOU CAN DO

You can do several things to make your child more comfortable, particularly if the pain develops in the middle of the night or your doctor can't see your child for several hours. Even when your doctor starts medication, it will not work immediately. Give fever and pain medicines such as acetaminophen (Tylenol, Tempra, etc.). Apply a warm cloth over the ear to soothe your child. If there is no drainage, use ear drops to temporarily reduce the pain.

If ear pain is due to a change in altitude, swallowing, chewing gum or blowing the nose hard while holding it closed may provide relief. For younger children, use a teething biscuit, pacifier or bottle.

After your doctor's visit, be sure to give all prescribed medicines and return for a recheck when scheduled.

Although there are multiple factors that produce ear pain, one way to help prevent infection is to prevent your child from drinking from a bottle while lying down.

VISITING YOUR CHILD'S DOCTOR

Your doctor will do a history and physical examination to make sure there is no serious problem besides the ear infection. Looking at the ear may make your child uncomfortable, but parents can help tremendously by reassuring their child and holding his/her arms and legs. After the examination, pick up and console your child. If there is a great deal of wax in your child's ear, ask your doctor for suggestions to reduce this problem in the future.

Your doctor will usually prescribe antibiotics, most of which are given two to three times per day by mouth. The type will depend on your child's age and the previous response, if any, to antibiotics. You will need to refrigerate some types. Your doctor will probably recheck your child's ear in two to three weeks and change the medicine if infection is still present. Decongestants are not useful unless your child has a bad runny nose.

If your child has recurrent ear infections, your doctor may prescribe daily low-dose medicines for several months to keep down infection. If this approach does not work or if there is a hearing loss, you may need to consult an ear specialist. A specialist can easily install ear tubes to assure proper drainage, if necessary.

If the problem is an infection of the ear canal only, ear drops alone are usually enough. Sometimes, particularly when the ear is draining, the middle ear and ear canal are also infected, requiring both antibiotics and ear drops.

Be sure to make arrangements for a follow-up appointment.

CAUTION

▼ Follow-up is essential to assure that long-term problems do not develop.

EYE REDNESS, DISCHARGE OR PAIN

An infection known as "pink eye" or conjunctivitis commonly causes redness, often with discharge. Eye irritation can also cause the same symptoms. Pain may indicate the presence of a foreign body or trauma to the eye.

WHAT to LOOK for

Commonly, there is a puslike discharge preceding or accompanying other respiratory symptoms such as runny nose, sore throat or low-grade fever. Often, the eye feels itchy and irritated. The discharge is sometimes thick and plentiful, causing the eye to crust over or become matted after sleeping. A thin discharge or none at all may occur if the problem is due to a virus, an allergy, an irritant in the air or a substance that comes in contact with the eye (chlorine in pool, make-up, etc.).

The eyelids are often slightly puffy and red. On occasion the eyelids and surrounding skin become red, swollen, firm and tender, indicating a skin infection.

Foreign bodies in the eye, such as small pieces of metal, dust or gravel cause a sharp, excruciating, localized pain. You can often see the material. A scratch of the cornea from something quickly touching the eye, such as a tree branch, causes a similar sensation.

WHEN to CALL YOUR CHILD'S DOCTOR

Call immediately if:

- Lid red and swollen;
- Eye pain;
- Impaired, blurred or double vision;
- Foreign body not easily removed;
- Injury to the eye, potential penetration or damage from a high-speed object;
- Chemical splashed in the eye;
- Eyeball cloudy, bloody or containing sores;
- Discharge from eye contains pus;
- Child is under one month old.

Call within a few hours if:

- Clear discharge or eye redness lasting over one week;
- Eyes do not improve after three days of medicine.

WHAT YOU CAN DO

Your doctor will usually prescribe some eye medicine. While your child is awake, clean the eye and use drops every two hours. To clean, gently remove the crusting with a warm, wet cotton ball. To administer drops, pull the lower lid down and place the drops in the lower lid gently. When the eye starts to improve, you can decrease the frequency to four times daily. For younger children, you may receive ointment instead of drops, which you use four times daily. Expect blurry vision with ointment. For bad or unresponsive infections, use the ointment at bedtime in conjunction with the drops.

Your child can infect other people. Use separate towels and washcloths and always wash hands carefully.

If an allergy or irritant caused your child's infection, try to avoid these substances. Often antihistamines, such as Benadryl (or equivalent), are helpful. If a chemical splashed in your child's eye, immediately wash the eye out very well and then call for advice.

If you think there may be a foreign object in the eye, pull down the lower lid and look, lifting the material off with a soft tissue. If it is still present, turn the upper eyelid back using a cotton swab and remove object, or pull the upper lid over the lower lid to remove the particle. Another approach is to rinse the eye with running water. If there is pain, your doctor should examine the eye.

VISITING YOUR CHILD'S DOCTOR

In most cases, your doctor will examine your child's eye and assess vision, movement and involvement of the lids. If it is "pink eye," medicine will be prescribed.

If there is a question of a foreign body, the eye will be further examined to identify any potential objects. Your doctor may try further steps to remove the material and, if unsuccessful, may refer your child to a specialist.

Occasionally, doctors place an orange substance in the eye and then examine the eye with a special light to be certain that there is no scratch. If a scratch is found, a tight patch is placed on the eye, and the eye is re-examined the next day to confirm healing.

CAUTION

▼ Marked prolonged pain, often associated with a foreign body, should be seen by an ophthalmologist.

FAINTING

Passing out or losing consciousness is frightening but usually resolves quickly in children.

WHAT to LOOK for

Children, and particularly adolescents, feel weak, light-headed and dizzy—sensations that may be followed rapidly by falling and a loss of consciousness. Closed or cramped spaces, stress, heat or hunger are common causes. Older children may be light-headed when standing up suddenly from a lying position, particularly after a prolonged medical procedure such as suturing.

Fainting or unconsciousness may occur after an injury to the head, drug overdose or convulsion (seizure).

On occasion, adolescents may breath rapidly and hyperventilate, with accompanying tingling of the fingers and lips. Such individuals may faint.

Breath-holding spells occur in children six months to four years old. After vigorous crying precipitated by a fall, injury or anger, some children become blue, unconscious and limp. These episodes usually last less than a minute, and the children quickly recover.

WHEN to CALL YOUR CHILD'S DOCTOR

Call immediately if:

- Unconscious or only partially awake;
- Head injury;
- Convulsion (seizure);
- Possible drug overdose.

Call within a few hours if:

- Fever;
- Persistent nausea, vomiting or dizziness;
- Headache;
- Recent onset of breath-holding spells.

Call for appointment if:

- Recurrent problem;
- Unusual stress or emotional upheaval.

WHAT YOU CAN DO

If your child faints or nearly faints in response to heat, crowding or stress, but quickly comes around, have him/her lie down and rest for a few minutes. Give your child orange juice or similar liquid containing sugar. Children who are feeling faint should avoid rapid changes in position.

If breathing is very fast, try to calm your child down. You may also have him/her breathe into cupped hands or a bag.

Children who hold their breath need special attention to avoid supporting this behavior. Firm and consistent limits are essential when attempting to minimize events and stresses that trigger the spells.

VISITING YOUR CHILD'S DOCTOR

A history and physical examination are particularly important in sorting out the nature of the fainting spell and deciding on additional tests. This information largely determines the nature of the visit.

CAUTION

▼ Fainting or unconsciousness following head injury, drug overdose or convulsion require urgent contact with your doctor.

FEVER

An elevated temperature is above 100.4° F (38.0° C) rectally, 99.7° F (37.6° C) orally or 99° F (37.2° C) axillary. Although infection is the most frequent cause, other factors may raise the temperature including food, excess clothing, anxiety, vigorous exercise or exposure to hot environments. When in doubt, take the temperature again in an hour.

Teething does not cause marked elevations in temperature. Immunizations, such as the DTP vaccine, can cause a transient fever during 24 to 48 hours following the injection.

WHAT to LOOK for

Fever is only one symptom of an infection; the important thing is to find out what is causing the temperature. Your child may also have ear pain, a sore throat, a runny nose, a cough, skin changes, vomiting and diarrhea.

Children with a high fever are often irritable or tired, with a flushed face and increased heart and breathing rates. Some children with very high temperatures hallucinate. These symptoms should improve when the temperature decreases; if they do not, your doctor should see your child.

Approximately 2 to 5 percent of normal children will have a convulsion with an elevated temperature. Convulsions usually occur with high temperatures and are indeed frightening; however, children usually recover from these episodes rapidly and without problems (see page 146).

WHEN to CALL YOUR CHILD'S DOCTOR

Call immediately if:

- Child is under three months old;
- Marked change in behavior with hallucinations, irritability, listlessness, sleepiness or crying without relief;
- Fever over 105° F (40.5° C) rectally;
- Looks sicker than expected, particularly after temperature decreases;
- Stiff neck, bad headache or convulsion (seizure);
- Fullness of soft spot in infant;
- Purple spots on skin;
- Difficulty breathing;
- Abdominal or belly pain;
- Dehydration (loss of water) with decreased urination, less moisture in diapers, dry mouth, no tears, weight loss, sleepiness or irritability.

Call within a few hours if:

- Fever over 103° F (39.5° C) in child under two years;
- Fever lasts longer than 48 hours;
- Burning on urination;
- Vomiting or diarrhea lasts longer than 12 hours.

WHAT YOU CAN DO

Taking your child's temperature is important. Take *rectal* temperatures as follows:

1. Shake the thermometer down below 96.8° F (36° C);
2. Lubricate with Vaseline, cold cream or cold water;
3. Gently insert the thermometer one-half inch into rectum. Hold your child still with his/her stomach down on your lap;
4. Leave in three minutes or until silver line stops rising;
5. Read the thermometer by turning the pointed edge of the triangle slightly in each direction until you identify the top of the mercury (silver) column;
6. On the Fahrenheit thermometer each line is 0.2° F, while on the centigrade (Celsius) thermometer each line is 0.1° C.

Take an *oral* temperature in the older child (generally at least five years old), by leaving the thermometer under the tongue for three minutes, provided that your child has had nothing to drink in the last 15 minutes. *Axillary* temperatures require that the thermometer be held under a dry armpit for four to six minutes. The elbow should be held against the chest.

Digital or electronic thermometers can simplify and shorten these procedures.

Fever medicines

Rectal temperatures below 101.5° F (38.6° C) do not need to be treated unless your child is very uncomfortable or a fever is present at bedtime. If your child is acting normally, fever medicines may be delayed until the temperature is 102.2° F (39.0° C).

Acetaminophen (Tylenol, Tempra, etc) is usually recommended every four to six hours by mouth. If your child's temperature is above 103° F (39.5° C) and does not come down quickly with acetaminophen (See table on page 166 for dosages), you may want to try sponging. Sponge your undressed child in lukewarm water (96 to 100° F). Many people prefer laying the undressed child on a towel. Another towel or washcloth soaked in lukewarm water is placed on the child and changed every one to two minutes. This is done for 15 to 30 minutes and repeated as often as necessary.

VISITING YOUR CHILD'S DOCTOR

If your child has a high fever, your doctor may prescribe additional fever medication. A full physical and history will often determine the type of infection and the appropriate treatment. Laboratory tests may be helpful.

CAUTION

- ▾ Persistent fever or fever in very young children requires a full medical evaluation to determine potential sites of infection as well as the need to begin treatment;
- ▾ Convulsions associated with fever may just be "febrile seizures," but infection of the nervous system must often be excluded.

TEMPERATURE EQUIVALENTS FOR RECTAL MEASUREMENTS

	F°		C°
Elevated	105.8	➡	41
Elevated	104.0	➡	40
Elevated	102.2	➡	39
Elevated	100.4	➡	38
Normal	98.6	➡	37

FEVER MEDICINE DOSAGE BY AGE*

0-3 mo	4-11 mo	12-23 mo	2-3 yr	4-5 yr	6-8 yr	9-10 yr	11-12 yr
Acetaminophen drops (80mg/0.8 ml)							
0.4 ml	0.8 ml	1.2 ml	1.6 ml	2.4 ml			
Acetaminophen elixir (160 mg/tsp.)							
	1/2 tsp	3/4 tsp	1 tsp	1 1/2 tsp	2 tsp	2 1/2 tsp	
Chewable tablet acetaminophen or aspirin (80 mg)							
		1 1/2	2	3	4	5	6
Junior swallowable tablet (160 mg)							
			1	1 1/2	2	2 1/2	3
Adult tablet acetaminophen or aspirin (325 mg)							
					1	1	1 1/2

*Your physician may recommend a higher dosage.

HEADACHE

Headache is a common problem in adolescents and adults; children under five years rarely have headaches without an underlying illness.

WHAT to LOOK for

In younger children, a headache may accompany common infections such as sore throat, earache, dental abcess or sinus problems. With viral infections, muscle ache and fever often accompany the headache. Accompanying fever and neck stiffness may indicate meningitis.

In older children and adolescents, stress and tension are

probably the most common causes of headaches accompanied by muscle spasms of the neck and head. The pain often worsens late in the day and may be constant, constricting or throbbing.

Throbbing, one-sided headaches are generally migraines. They have a relatively rapid onset and in many patients cause severe pain with nausea, vomiting, belly pain and eye problems. Another family member may have similar types of headaches.

Convulsions or head trauma may precede the onset. Carbon monoxide poisoning due to exposure from an unvented furnace, fire, etc., may produce headaches. Impaired vision is rarely a cause.

WHEN to CALL YOUR CHILD'S DOCTOR

Call immediately if:

- Severe, persistent pain;
- Stiff neck;
- Marked behavioral change with irritability or sleepiness;
- Unequal pupils;
- Evidence of problems including confusion, impaired speech or vision or recurrent vomiting;
- Traumatic head injury;
- Child under five years old.

Call within a few hours if:

- Persistent headache lasts longer than 48 to 72 hours;
- Fever without any other symptoms;
- Wakes child up from sleep or lasts for more than 24 hours.

Call for an appointment if:

- Recurrent headaches;
- Problems with friends, family or school.

WHAT YOU CAN DO

The main goal of treatment of minor headaches is to try to minimize the pain and return to normal function. Initiate treatment as recommended by your physician.

Stress is the most common cause of headaches. Treatment may include rest, massage and counseling to reorient priorities.

VISITING YOUR CHILD'S DOCTOR

Your doctor will determine the pattern and type of your child's headaches, following a normal physical exam. Your doctor will give particular attention to the nervous system.

If there is any concern about the particular pattern of headaches in your child, it will be important to run tests to exclude other frequent causes.

If there is any head or neck trauma, specific X-ray studies may indicate potential problems.

CAUTION

▼ Headaches in infants require evaluation to determine contributing factors.

HEAT EXPOSURE (HYPERTHERMIA)

Too much exposure to heat due to weather, exercise or working in a closed, hot space can create problems that are preventable.

WHAT to LOOK for

Heat cramps are due to sweating during prolonged exercise in a setting that is hot with low humidity. Severe cramps develop in the muscles, particularly the legs.

Heat exhaustion (prostration) results from exposure combined with not taking enough fluids and salt to replace those lost from continuous sweating in a hot environment. Children are often dehydrated; the skin appears pale and clammy. They are usually weak, thirsty and irritable, with nausea and headache. Body temperature is relatively normal.

Heat stroke is the least common but most significant reaction to prolonged heat exposure and exertion. Common symptoms include nausea, vomiting, headache, fatigue, confusion and disorientation. The skin is red, hot and dry, and the body temperature is often above 105° F (40° C).

WHEN to CALL YOUR CHILD'S DOCTOR

Call immediately if:

- High fever;
- Red, hot and dry skin;
- Confusion or disorientation;
- Rapid pulse.

Call within a few hours if:

- Weakness, thirst, nausea or irritability persist after taking fluids.

WHAT YOU CAN DO

To reduce muscle cramps, give fluids and allow your child to rest. If available, you may want to give your child water with a few shakes (one-half teaspoon) of table salt per glass every 15 to 30 minutes as tolerated. Drinking a great deal of fluid before initiating prolonged play, work or exercise in a hot environment can prevent cramps, particularly if the fluid is supplemented by eating salty foods.

Heat exhaustion responds to rest in a cool place and salt water (one-half teaspoon of table salt per glass) or other cool fluids such as Gatorade. Most children quickly feel better. If your child does not improve after three to four glasses, your doctor may want to do a full evaluation.

Heat stroke is potentially dangerous, as children are dehydrated and have high temperatures. Begin steps to bring the temperature down by taking your child to a cool place. Sponge with cool water and fan your child while sprinkling him/her with cold water. If your child is conscious, give cold water with one-half teaspoon of table salt per glass. Arrange rapid transport to an emergency facility.

VISITING YOUR CHILD'S DOCTOR

All patients with evidence of heat stroke should have the temperature brought down rapidly and fluids restored. Blood tests provide information about the seriousness of the problem. Hospitalization is usually necessary.

With other heat-related conditions, your doctor should see your child if there is not a rapid response.

The key to this problem is prevention. Adequate water and salt intake combined with appropriate acclimatization and equipment are required.

CAUTION

▼ Children with elevated temperatures following heat exposure need careful evaluation, fluids and external means of reducing the temperature.

HYPOTHERMIA AND FROSTBITE

Children may lose heat from prolonged exposure to cold, leading to a very low body temperature.

WHAT to LOOK for

The seriousness depends on the extent and duration of the lowered body temperature. Initially, children shiver. Slurred speech, confusion, disorientation, muscle stiffness, poor coordination and blueness follow. Ultimately, children with temperatures below 86° F (30° C) may become unconscious and develop heart problems. Special low-reading thermometers are needed to accurately determine such low temperatures.

Frostbite may occur, particularly on the hands, feet, toes, ears and nose. The severity depends on the absolute temperature, the length of exposure, the wind-chill factor and the degree of mobility. With minimal frostbite, the skin is red and swollen with burning and tingling. It may then become white and pale. As the area thaws, a dull, aching pain may occur. Worse problems occur when the skin develops blisters or becomes markedly swollen with skin breakdown.

WHEN to CALL YOUR CHILD'S DOCTOR

Call immediately if:

- Temperature is below 94° F (34.4° C);
- Unconscious, confused or disoriented;
- Irregular pulse or breathing;
- Other medical problems;
- Frostbite with blisters, swelling or skin breakdown.

Call within a few hours if:

- Symptoms remain when temperature is raised;
- Temperature not easily raised above 95° F (35° C).

WHAT YOU CAN DO

Of primary importance is to place your child in a warm environment. Warmed blankets and heated objects (hot water bottle, etc.) may be applied to the chest and sides, being careful not to cause burns.

Rewarm frostbitten skin carefully. Avoid refreezing. If the frostbite is superficial, hold fingers or toes in the armpits; other areas may be warmed by blowing on them with hot air. Do not rub the affected area. If the frostbite is more severe, immerse involved areas in tepid water (104 to 109° F or 40.5 to 43.3° C) for 20 minutes and then wrap in gauze and keep elevated. Pain medicines may be needed. Handle involved area gently.

Appropriate clothing and equipment will usually prevent problems from exposure.

VISITING YOUR CHILD'S DOCTOR

Body temperature below 94° F (34.4° C) requires active steps to speed up the rewarming, while checking to be certain that no problems develop. Children with deep frostbite need careful evaluation of the involved area.

CAUTION

▼ Severe hypothermia requires immediate steps to rewarm the affected area.

IRRITABILITY

Children may be irritable from a vast array of causes, the actual change in behavior often being a symptom of some underlying problem.

WHAT to LOOK for

Irritability commonly accompanies infections, particularly when your child also has a fever, sore throat, ear pain, muscle ache or headache. Immunizations, especially DTP vaccine, can cause changes in behavior.

In the infant between two weeks and three months old, colic is the most common cause of persistent crying and irritability, and usually occurs late in the afternoon or evening. The child is healthy between episodes.

Teething often begins at about six months, resulting in irritated, swollen gums as teeth erupt. High fever, significant diarrhea or marked diaper rashes do not accompany teething and thus indicate different problems.

Rarely, your child can be injured without you being aware of it. Your child will usually complain of pain when you touch a bone or move a joint. Look for a string or hair wrapped around a toe or finger or a splinter imbedded in the skin.

Decongestants and asthma medicines can cause anxiety and irritability in children. Lastly, your child may be irritable in response to anxiety, concerns, stresses or pressures within your family.

WHEN to CALL YOUR CHILD'S DOCTOR

Call immediately if:

- Behavioral change in an inconsolable child;
- Behavioral change persisting beyond six hours without any definable cause;
- High fever;
- Worrisome signs or symptoms;
- Your frustration with your child's irritability is increasing.

WHAT YOU CAN DO

If there are no signs of infection such as an ear infection, or a sore throat, look over your child carefully for sources of injury or irritation. Eliminate all medications, if they are not essential. Try to be reassuring and minimize stress.

VISITING YOUR CHILD'S DOCTOR

Your doctor will take a thorough history and do a careful physical examination. If the evaluation is normal, tests may offer further reassurance. The first visit may not provide an answer; your doctor may suggest trying different approaches at home and may arrange a return visit.

CAUTION

▼ The irritable child may have an illness that needs evaluation and treatment. Often there are underlying behavioral problems.

KIDNEY OR BLADDER INFECTION (Urinary tract infections or UTIs)

Infections of the urinary tract may involve the kidney or the bladder. They are more common in girls.

WHAT to LOOK for

Urinary tract infections commonly cause painful (burning), frequent or bloody urination. Children may also have belly and back pain, fever, chills, nausea, vomiting and a general sense of weakness and malaise.

Girls may pass small amounts of urine or have a sense of burning on urination because of irritation, not infection. This can be due to bubble baths, trauma, masturbation or incorrect wiping (correct wiping is from front to back). Girls may have a vaginal discharge.

Blood in the urine may indicate a problem with the kidney not caused by infection.

Toilet-trained younger children may resume bed-wetting, usually in response to a new or increasing stress rather than infection.

WHEN to CALL YOUR CHILD'S DOCTOR

Call immediately if:

- Severe abdominal or back pain;
- High fever or chills;
- Blood in urine;
- Unable to pass urine;
- Swollen eyes, weight increase, headaches or decreased urination.

Call within a few hours if:

- Painful burning or frequent urination;
- Previous problems with urinary tract infections;
- Pain and other symptoms do not improve within 48 hours of beginning antibiotics;
- Medicines not tolerated.

Call for an appointment if:

- Recent onset of bed-wetting in child without other symptoms.

WHAT YOU CAN DO

In girls, irritation commonly causes burning and frequent urination and may quickly be resolved by soaking in a tub of clean water with one-half cup of vinegar (without soap) for about 20 minutes. Repeat for a few days. To prevent the recurrence of the problem, use bubble bath and soap sparingly, if at all. Often, to resolve the problem, showers should be substituted for baths. Encourage wiping from front to back, and use white cotton underpants. Avoid constipation. If there are other symptoms or an infection is possible, see your doctor.

After evaluation and prescription of antibiotics by your doctor, treat the infection at home. Give medicines for the entire prescribed course. Even when your child is feeling better, he/she may still have the infection. Follow-up visits are necessary to prevent or monitor recurrences.

VISITING YOUR CHILD'S DOCTOR

Your doctor will examine your child for abdominal and back pain and will evaluate the genital area for irritation.

Your doctor will do a microscopic examination of a urine specimen and, if necessary, a culture. For younger children, you may use a bag to collect the urine. For older children, your doctor will need a clean sample. To obtain a clean sample from girls, wash the genital area several times with warm water and cotton. While your child is sitting on a toilet with her legs spread, have her urinate and collect some urine midstream (i.e., not at the beginning or the end of the stream). Boys should similarly have midstream urine collected. If done at home, keep the specimen refrigerated in a sterile jar until your doctor's visit.

If your child has an infection, your doctor will begin antibiotics and will make arrangements for follow-up.

If no infection is present, irritation is the most likely cause and preventive steps noted above will be reviewed.

Bed-wetting may require visits to your doctor to develop an understanding of the contributing factors.

CAUTION

▾ Painful (burning) or frequent urination requires evaluation to exclude infection.

LIMPING

Children walk abnormally or limp because of problems with the leg bones, hips, knees or back.

WHAT to LOOK for

Children with a limp usually have an injury or other problem. Determine which leg hurts and examine for tenderness along the bone or upon movement of the ankle, knee or hip. The joint or bone may have overlying redness, swelling and tenderness. Hip problems can cause knee pain. Children with belly problems and pain from a condition, such as appendicitis, may also have a limp.

Make certain that there is no splinter, cut or other injury to the foot. Many viral illnesses, such as German measles (rubella), can cause painful joints. Infection of the bone or joint can occur. Hairline (small) fractures are often difficult to detect.

Toxic synovitis of the hip is the most common cause of unexplained limp in children 18 months to seven years old. Often a viral illness precedes; however, children are not sick and rarely complain of any discomfort.

WHEN to CALL YOUR CHILD'S DOCTOR

Call immediately if:

- Pain of bone or joint;
- Fever or toxicity.

Call within a few hours if:

- Limp persists for more than four hours;
- Limitation of movement of joint or leg;
- Trauma to leg.

WHAT YOU CAN DO

Have your child evaluated. Toxic synovitis requires careful monitoring of your child combined with rest. Bacterial infection, although rare, requires prolonged therapy and hospitalization.

VISITING YOUR CHILD'S DOCTOR

After considering the contributing factors, your doctor will assess all of the extremities for range of motion and possible bone involvement and will try to exclude infection and trauma. Blood tests and X-rays are often helpful in worrisome circumstances.

Joint or bone infection usually requires hospitalization. Occasionally, your doctor may consult an orthopedist.

CAUTION

▾ Limping in a child requires rapid evaluation.

MUMPS

Mumps is a viral infection of the salivary glands. There is an excellent vaccine against it. The period between exposure and illness (incubation period) is about 14 to 21 days. Children are infectious until the parotid gland swelling disappears.

WHAT to LOOK for

Children have swelling of the salivary glands, most commonly the parotid gland located just in front of and below the ears. Chewing lemons or pickles make the pain worse. A low-grade fever and headache may accompany swelling. There is no rash.

Problems may include swelling and pain of the testicles as well as inflammation of the brain or pancreas.

WHEN to CALL YOUR CHILD'S DOCTOR

Call immediately if:

- Convulsions, sleepiness.

Call with a few hours if:

- Pain or swelling of testicle(s);
- Abdominal pain or vomiting;
- Swollen lymph nodes ("glands") of the neck.

WHAT YOU CAN DO

Reduce discomfort with acetaminophen. Encourage fluids and avoid sour substances and citrus fruits. If testicular pain develops, rest, support and pain medicines are usually adequate. Check to be certain that your other children are immunized.

VISITING YOUR CHILD'S DOCTOR

After assuring that the illness is mumps (as opposed to swollen lymph nodes), your doctor will examine your child for complications and will suggest specific measures, if necessary.

NECK PAIN AND SWELLING

Pain or swelling of the neck commonly occurs with infection or injury to the neck.

WHAT to LOOK for

Children complaining of neck pain or swelling usually have swollen lymph nodes ("glands") due to a sore throat or other infection of the airway. Streptococcal infection is a common cause, particularly when the lymph nodes are tender with overlying redness of the skin.

Small nodes in the back of the head, behind the ears and in the neck region are common in children. Nodes often enlarge in response to a small cut, abrasion or infection. This can occur not only with nodes in the neck but in other areas such as the groin, armpit or elbow.

A high fever, difficulty touching the chin to the chest, marked behavioral changes, discomfort with swallowing, difficulty breathing or drooling may indicate more serious infection.

An injury with neck pain, any loss of sensation or strength, or pains shooting into the arm requires immobilization of the neck. These symptoms commonly follow accidents in automobiles or on trampolines. Do not move your child until it can be done safely, usually using a hard board and taping the head with the assistance of ambulance personnel.

In infancy, pressure on the neck during delivery often produces bleeding in the muscle with swelling and pain on movement. When older children pull a neck muscle, they develop a stiff neck known as torticollis or wry neck.

WHEN to CALL YOUR CHILD'S DOCTOR

Call immediately if:

- Neck trauma (do not move without immobilization). Usually call 911;
- High fever, difficulty touching chin to chest or behavioral change;
- Drooling or difficulty breathing;
- Discomfort with swallowing;
- Stiff neck without tenderness;
- Extreme pain.

Call within a few hours if:

- Lymph nodes ("glands") are tender or larger than three inches or if overlying skin is red;
- Fever over 102° F (39° C) or any elevated temperature lasting longer than 24 hours;
- Sore throat or ear pain;
- Pain lasting more than 48 hours.

WHAT YOU CAN DO

Treat muscle spasm or injury with heating pads and massage combined with mild pain-relief and muscle-relaxation medication in older children. Recurrent problems in an older child may require specific physical therapy.

Most large nodes caused by infections, particularly when they are tender with overlying redness, are due to streptococcus and respond to antibiotics. Use acetaminophen (Tylenol, Tempra, etc.) for fever control. The nodes commonly become nontender after 24 to 36 hours. They may remain large for weeks or months.

Immediately immobilize a traumatized or injured child who has neck pain. Logroll (DO NOT LIFT) your child onto a stiff board and tape his/her head down. Keep your child calm by offering reassurance, talking and stroking his/her head.

VISITING YOUR CHILD'S DOCTOR

After careful examination of the neck, your doctor will decide if the problem is injury or infection. Different types of infection require different treatments, often combined with antibiotics. Your doctor may exclude serious infections by using special tests.

If the pain is due to trauma with muscle spasm, the neck, collarbone or shoulder may require X-ray studies. If there is no bone damage, your doctor may make suggestions for relieving your child's discomfort.

CAUTION

▼ A child with a nontender stiff neck, difficulty breathing, or high fever often has a serious infection requiring immediate evaluation.

▼ Never move a child with neck trauma or injury and neck pain until it can be done safely.

POISONING

Most accidental poisoning occurs in children who are under five years old. In those under one year, poisoning is usually due to parental mistakes in giving medicines. Older children are adventuresome and curious, sporadically experimenting with any products and medications they may find.

WHAT YOU CAN DO

Children who ingest either potentially dangerous substances or excessive amounts of normally safe products require careful examination.

Make sure your child is acting and breathing normally (see earlier section on page 109).

Flush exposed area or induce vomiting.

Skin exposed to acids, caustics or insecticides should be flooded with water and washed with soap. Remove all contaminated clothing.

Eyes exposed to acids or caustics should be washed immediately for 15 to 20 minutes before taking your child to your doctor. Hold your child's head under running water in a sink or shower or pour water into the eye from a pitcher or a glass.

Taken by mouth: Vomiting should be induced using syrup of ipecac in children over six months of age in the following amounts:

Six to 12 month-old: Give two teaspoons
One to 12 year-old: Give three teaspoons (one-half ounce)
Over 12 years: Give six teaspoons (one ounce)

It is often valuable to call your poison-control center before giving syrup of ipecac, since the poisoning may not be serious and may require no therapy.

If syrup of ipecac is given, encourage your child to drink water or clear liquids and to walk around, if possible. Give another dose of syrup of ipecac if your child does not vomit after 20 minutes. If necessary, a throat stick, spoon or finger at the back of the throat may be helpful.

DO NOT USE syrup of ipecac if your child has taken acid or caustics such as strong household cleaners, lye, strong bleach, etc. Give your child water or milk to dilute the substance and call your doctor or poison center or get immediate medical attention.

DO NOT USE syrup of ipecac if your child is sleepy or unresponsive.

Call your regional poison-control center!
(Fill in with your area's number.) Phone__________________

This is probably the quickest place to receive advice on the nature of the substance your child has taken and the severity of the poisoning. You should review your plans with the center and arrange for your doctor or the nearest emergency department to see your child.

Take your child to a hospital or to a doctor!

In most cases your child should be seen by your doctor or an emergency department unless the poison control center says the ingested substance(s) was not toxic or dangerous. To permit an accurate identification, take the container with the medication or substance ingested with you.

Prevent poisoning (see Ch. 5).

Dangerous household substances, such as medications, dishwasher soap, cleaning supplies, drain-cleaning crystals or liquids, paints and thinners, automobile products and garden sprays, must be put away in locked cabinets. Always keep medications in child-proof containers! Be particularly watchful during periods of disruptions such as moving, travel, visitors, etc. Often grandparents have medications in a container, purse or piece of baggage that is not child-proof.

Have syrup of ipecac in the house for emergencies.

VISITING YOUR CHILD'S DOCTOR

Your doctor will determine if there is any problem with breathing or responsiveness. Appropriate steps will be taken to stabilize your child.

Your doctor will wash the eye or skin, if involved.

Your child's stomach will be emptied if this has not already occurred. This is done by making your child vomit or by putting a tube through the nose or mouth into the stomach and rinsing out the stomach. Your doctor will then give charcoal and a cathartic to further absorb and eliminate the ingested substance. Your doctor may check blood levels to measure the severity of the poisoning.

Hospitalization may be necessary, depending on the ingested substances, the potential complications and the reason for the poisoning. Poison prevention activities will be reviewed.

If your child is sent home, *call back* if your child develops any worrisome problems that were reviewed during your visit.

RASHES

Rashes in children come in many sizes, colors and shapes. It is hard to distinguish different types of skin problems; the following list may help sort out some of the more common ones:

Rashes that are red without bumps

Measles (Rubeola)
Rubella (German or three-day measles)
Roseola
Scarlet fever
Drug (ampicillin) rash
Erythema infectiosum (Fifth disease)
"Viral rash"

Rashes that are red with bumps

Acne
Candidiasis (monila diaper rash)
Contact dermatitis
Diaper rash
Eczema
Hives
Impetigo
Insect bite
Ringworm

Rashes with blisters (fluid-filled)

Chicken pox (Varicella)
Herpes zoster
Impetigo, bullous
Insect bite
Scabies

Rashes that are purple or red without blanching (i.e., when the skin is pulled tight between two fingers, rash still appears red or purple). There are virtually always emergencies.

Bacterial infection in blood

CALL YOUR CHILD'S DOCTOR if you are uncertain what kind of rash your child has or if there are problems.

Call immediately if:

- Purple, red or blood-like without blanching;
- Burn-like;
- Red, blue or tender to the touch;
- Red-streaking;
- Pustular.

Call within a few hours if:

- Skin is itchy;
- Child looks sick;
- Fever last over 24 hours;
- Rash related to medications;
- Pustules present with red or cola-colored urine.

If the rash concerns you, your child appears to be sick or the rash persists, you should call your doctor because identifying rashes is difficult.

The following pages provide information about the more common rashes. However, rashes and their accompanying illnesses rarely look exactly as described, and you should generally see your doctor to confirm your suspicions.

RASH—ACNE

Acne is common in 85 percent of adolescents. It is caused by hormonal changes occurring at puberty that produce a blockage of hair follicles and oil glands.

WHAT to LOOK for

Pimples are common, usually on the face, upper chest and back. Adolescents get "blackheads" from follicle openings filling with pigmented material. Blockage of follicles causes a collection of secretions or cysts known as "whiteheads."

WHEN to CALL YOUR CHILD'S DOCTOR

Call for an appointment if:

- Unattractive or bothersome;
- Painful cysts or drainage.

WHAT YOU CAN DO

Keeping the face clean is important. Have your child scrub his/her face several times daily with a mild soap (Neutrogena or Dove). Agents such as benzoyl peroxide (Desquamex or Benzagel) or retinoic acid (Retin A) when used once a day, initially can help peel the skin with less plugging of follicles. If this does not produce improvement, your doctor may prescribe antibiotics.

Your child should avoid all cosmetics; if they are necessary, use only water-soluble products. Particular foods do not generally play a role in making acne worse. The problem may worsen in the winter and, for girls, just before menstrual periods.

VISITING YOUR CHILD'S DOCTOR

Your doctor will work with you to develop a plan; don't be discouraged, since it takes weeks to months to see marked improvement. The goal is to control the acne.

RASH—CHICKEN POX (Varicella)

Chicken pox is an infection caused by a virus. The time between exposure to someone with chicken pox and the beginning of the illness (incubation period) is 14 to 21 days. Children are infectious from one day before the rash appears until the blisters dry and crust over (seven days). It spreads very easily.

WHAT to LOOK for

Rash

Look for a sudden onset of flat, red spots that become small, raised bumps and finally small blisters surrounded by a red area. The rash is primarily on the trunk and is very itchy, tending to appear in groups of lesions in different stages. After the blisters break, they scab over and form a crust. Some children have only a few lesions while others are totally covered.

Other

Preceding the rash, there are usually no symptoms except for an occasional fever which may persist during the illness. Lesions may become infected, producing impetigo. Rarely, patients may develop a lung infection or have impaired responsiveness.

WHEN to CALL YOUR CHILD'S DOCTOR

Call immediately if:

- Marked toxicity or your child looks very ill;
- Rapid or difficult breathing;
- Convulsion, sleepiness or severe headache;
- Underlying disease in your child.

Call within a few hours if:

- Lesions get red, warm, tender or drain pus;
- Your newborn is exposed to chicken pox.

WHAT YOU CAN DO

Keep your child comfortable. Give baking soda baths (one-half cup in tub) to soothe. Use Calamine lotion on the skin. Cut fingernails to minimize scratching. If your child is having trouble drinking, have him/her gargle with salt water. If the throat is still sore, have your child gargle with an antacid like Mylanta or Maalox to coat the mouth.

Start antihistamines, such as Benadryl, for severe itching. Do not use aspirin. Keep your child out of day care or school until the blisters crust over.

VISITING YOUR CHILD'S DOCTOR

Rarely is a visit required unless there are specific, worrisome problems.

RASH—CONTACT DERMATITIS

Skin irritants can cause rashes. Typical substances include alkali, detergents, plants (poison ivy and poison oak), medicine put on the skin, shoes, nickel and cosmetics.

WHAT to LOOK for

The skin is red and swollen; blisters and crusts may form. The distribution of the rash follows the pattern of contact.

WHEN to CALL YOUR CHILD'S DOCTOR

Call within a few hours if:

- Weepy, blistery lesion with swelling.

WHAT YOU CAN DO

No therapy is usually necessary except for avoiding the irritating substance. If the irritation is extensive, hydration of the skin may help. After baths, apply a mild lotion, such as Eucerin or Nivea before drying your child off. Another alternative is to apply towels or cloths moistened with warm water to weeping areas to clear up the involved region.

If the problem is particularly bothersome, applying steroid cream (hydrocortisone) to the area may hasten healing.

Avoid future contact with the offending substance.

VISITING YOUR CHILD'S DOCTOR

If the problem is severe, your doctor may prescribe special medicine to decrease the swelling and irritation.

RASH—DIAPER DERMATITIS AND CANDIDIASIS

Prolonged contact between skin and urine or stool in the diaper area produces irritation and dampness. This may lead to additional irritation from *Candida*.

WHAT to LOOK for

The diaper area is red, with small blisters or areas of minor ulcer. If small, red areas with bumps are present, often in areas of creases appearing as "kissing lesions," the child also has *monilia* which is due to an infection of *Candida*. Many children with monilia also have red areas with white patches on the inside of the mouth, which is known as *thrush*.

WHEN to CALL YOUR CHILD'S DOCTOR

Call for an appointment if:

- No improvement with home treatment;
- Red areas with bumps along creases.

WHAT YOU CAN DO

Keep the diaper area clean by changing diapers frequently and cleaning the area each time using warm water. Occasionally, mild soaps will help such as Neutrogena, Basis, Lowila or Cetaphil.

Leave your child without a diaper as much as possible, particularly during naps. Fasten diapers loosely. If you use cloth diapers, double-rinse them. Do not use plastic pants. If you use disposable diapers, punch a few holes in the plastic liner. Sometimes children do better with one brand of diapers rather than another. You may want to try several brands.

If there are red areas with bumps along the creases, you may need to apply special cream to the involved areas at diaper changes. If there are white areas in your child's mouth, you may give a similar oral medication by mouth that can be prescribed by your doctor.

VISITING YOUR CHILD'S DOCTOR

Only rarely do children with a diaper rash need to visit the doctor. If the rash is bad or difficult to treat, your doctor can prescribe special medication to hasten healing.

RASH—ECZEMA OR ATOPIC DERMATITIS

Eczema is often present with other allergic conditions and is at least partially due to an inability to retain moisture in the skin, i.e., the skin is too dry. There may be a family history of allergies.

WHAT to LOOK for

Skin is red, dry and scaly, involving areas of irritation on the body as well as the face. Involved areas are usually symmetrically distributed and become progressively red and swollen with crusting and weeping. Children usually itch. Infection with crusting and pus occurs occasionally.

WHEN to CALL YOUR CHILD'S DOCTOR

Call within a few hours if:

- Marked redness, crusting or weepy lesions;
- Infection with crusting or pus.

Call for an appointment if:

- No response to therapy.

WHAT YOU CAN DO

In mild disease without significant weeping or crusting, try to hydrate the skin. Bathe your child and then apply Eucerin lotion to involved areas without drying the skin. Do not use soap. If there is a small area with marked redness, a steroid cream such as hydrocortisone, may be used for one to two days.

Moderate problems require more active steps for two to three days. Apply a towel or cloth dampened with warm water to the involved areas. Remove, rewet and reapply towels every five minutes for a total of three treatments. Repeat three times daily. At night, bathe your child, put on damp cotton pajamas and then cover with a second, dry pair. If necessary, use a steroid cream as well as antihistamines, such as Benadryl to reduce itching.

After the skin has improved, improve hydration with daily baths and applications of Eucerin to the wet skin without drying off your child. In mild cases, use lubricating creams such as Nivea. Do not use soap; Cetaphil lotion is a good soap substitute. Keep fingernails short.

VISITING YOUR CHILD'S DOCTOR

After examining your child, your doctor will review the plan and make additional suggestions. If the condition is serious, your doctor may recommend hospitalization.

RASH—ERYTHEMA INFECTIOSUM (Fifth Disease)

Fifth disease is a common viral disease. The period between exposure to others with the illness and development of a rash (incubation period) is about seven to 14 days.

WHAT to LOOK for

Initially the cheeks are red and flushed ("slapped cheek"), which may spread to become a lacelike eruption on the arms and legs. It may recur with heat, sunlight or trauma.

WHEN to CALL YOUR CHILD'S DOCTOR

Call for an appointment if:

- Anxiety or concern about rash.

WHAT YOU CAN DO

Since children are not ill, they should not need to visit your doctor except for an identification of the rash.

RASH—HIVES (or Urticaria)

Hives are an allergic reaction to substances such as food, medicines, insect bites, etc.

WHAT to LOOK for

Rash

Red, raised lesions with marked swelling that are often itchy. They are often called "welts."

Ampicillin and amoxicillin commonly causes a rash, which may be related to an allergy but more commonly is not. The nonallergenic rash consists of small bumps with a slightly red base appearing seven to 10 days after beginning the medicine. Allergic problems begin in the first four to five days.

Other

Difficult or rapid breathing.

WHEN to CALL YOUR CHILD'S DOCTOR

Call immediately if:

- Difficult or rapid breathing.

Call within a few hours if:

- Bothersome itching.

WHAT YOU CAN DO

If the itching is bothersome, antihistamines, such as Benadryl, may be useful. If there are associated problems, the adequacy of the airway and breathing must be assessed immediately.

It is important to exclude things that cause problems such as drugs, eggs, milk, chocolate, shellfish, cheese, nuts, pollens and insect bites.

VISITING YOUR CHILD'S DOCTOR

A visit is only required if there is difficulty breathing. Your doctor needs to administer medications quickly to reverse the process.

RASH—IMPETIGO

Impetigo is a superficial infection of the skin that occurs with cuts, abrasions or irritation of the skin. It is more frequent in the summer.

WHAT to LOOK for

Rash

Small, red areas quickly develop blisters and then form a honey-colored crust. They may spread. Large blisters that grow together may also appear. The face, arms, legs and areas of abrasion are most commonly involved.

Other

Rarely, the kidney is involved, producing a gray, cola-colored urine.

WHEN to CALL YOUR CHILD'S DOCTOR

Call within a few hours if:

- Blisters are crusting over;
- No response to medicines;
- Cola-colored urine.

WHAT YOU CAN DO

Scrub and soak the involved area to try to loosen or dissolve any crusts that have formed. Antibiotics will not cure the problem unless the crusts are removed. Give all doses of medicine until the prescription is completely finished. Minimize sharing of towels, sheets, etc.

VISITING YOUR CHILD'S DOCTOR

After making the diagnosis, your doctor will prescribe antibiotics and will give you instructions about removing crusts and keeping your child clean.

RASH—LICE

Lice are small insects that are usually found in the head and genital areas. People transmit them to other people.

WHAT to LOOK for

Small, raised bumps are present in the head or genital area. "Nits" (lice eggs) may also be found in these areas. There is usually a great deal of associated itching.

WHEN to CALL YOUR CHILD'S DOCTOR

Call for an appointment if:

- Severe itching, particularly if no response to home management.

WHAT YOU CAN DO

Several products are available, some without a prescription, that should kill the lice. RID and NIX are common, as is Kwell shampoo. Apply RID undiluted to the infested area, allow to remain for 10 minutes and then wash off thoroughly. Give a second treatment in seven to 10 days. For Kwell shampoo, apply to the area and work into a lather with water for four minutes and then wash thoroughly. Treat others who have a similar rash and have had contact with your child, if they are not pregnant.

You can comb out nits. Washing the hair with diluted, warm vinegar makes this easier. If the eyebrows or lashes are involved, apply petrolatum (Vaseline) carefully to the area overnight.

Wash your child's bed linens and clothes that have been worn recently. For four days don't allow your child to wear hats and other headgear that are difficult to wash. Use antihistamines, such as Benadryl, if itching is a problem.

VISITING YOUR CHILD'S DOCTOR

Rarely, a visit is needed to confirm the diagnosis.

RASH—MEASLES

Measles is a very contagious, viral infection that is uncommon today because an excellent vaccine exists. The incubation period (time between exposure and beginning of illness) is 10 to 14 days.

WHAT to LOOK for

Rash

A reddish, blotchy, flat rash develops after several days of illness. It begins on the face and goes downward, spreading to the chest and abdomen and finally the arms and legs. The rash lasts for seven days, may turn brownish in color and often peels.

Other

Children are usually sick, beginning with a high fever, cough, pink eye and runny nose. These symptoms develop before the rash appears. Classically, children have a red area with fine white spots opposite the molars. Other problems that may develop include a sore throat or infection of the ear, lung or lining of the brain.

WHEN to CALL YOUR CHILD'S DOCTOR

Call immediately if:

- Marked toxicity (child appears very ill);
- Rapid or difficult breathing;
- Seizure, listlessness or headache.

Call within a few hours if:

- Persistent high fever beyond five days;
- Ear pain;
- Your newborn is exposed;
- Underlying disease.

WHAT YOU CAN DO

It is important to make your child comfortable. Use fever medicines (acetaminophen). Push fluids in small amounts and do not worry if your child is uninterested in taking solids. Avoid bright lights. Rarely is cough or eye medicine necessary.

Make sure your other children are immunized.

VISITING YOUR CHILD'S DOCTOR

A history and physical will determine if there are any complications. Children with bad lung infections or marked changes in behavior or alertness may require hospitalization.

Your other children may receive gamma globulin if they are not otherwise protected.

Arrange for immunization of other children if necessary.

RASH—RINGWORM

Ringworm is a skin infection caused by a fungus.

WHAT to LOOK for

The lesions start as small, round, red spots and slowly get larger with a scaly outer rim and a relatively clear center. They are most common on the face, arms, shoulders, or groin and may be itchy. Infection may develop.

WHEN to CALL YOUR CHILD'S DOCTOR

Call for an appointment if:

- Lesions get red, warm, tender or drain pus;
- Scalp or nails are involved;
- No improvement. Spreading after a week of medicine.

WHAT YOU CAN DO

Purchase tinactin (or similar) cream, available without a prescription, and apply to the involved areas two times daily for up to several weeks. Continue the medicine for a week after the problem has cleared up.

VISITING YOUR CHILD'S DOCTOR

If the lesions are not going away, your doctor will probably scrape a small sample of the scales, look at them under a microscope to confirm the diagnosis and prescribe other medicines. Infections of the scalp or nails require special medications taken for a prolonged period.

RASH—ROSEOLA (Exanthema Subitum)

Roseola is a viral infection that occurs most frequently in children six to 12 months old. The period between exposure and beginning of illness is 10 to 14 days.

WHAT to LOOK for

Rash

The rose-colored rash appears after the fever disappears. It is initially on the chest and then spreads to the face, arms and legs. It disappears quickly.

Other

A high fever occurs for the first three to four days followed by a rash as the temperature returns to normal. Convulsions may occur, particularly during the period of high fever.

WHEN to CALL YOUR CHILD'S DOCTOR

Call immediately if:

- Convulsions.

Call within a few hours if:

- High fever with accompanying symptoms.

WHAT YOU CAN DO

Make your child feel comfortable. Keep his/her temperature down with fever medicines (aspirin or acetaminophen).

VISITING YOUR CHILD'S DOCTOR

Your doctor will make certain that there is no other problem complicating the illness.

RASH—RUBELLA (German Measles or Three-Day Measles)

Rubella is a viral infection that is less common now because there is an excellent vaccine. The incubation period (time between exposure and onset of symptoms) is 14 to 21 days. Children remain infectious from seven days before the rash appears until five days after the rash appears. If your child has come in contact with a pregnant woman, the woman should contact her physician immediately.

WHAT to LOOK for

Rash

The pink rash begins on the face as flat or slightly raised red spots and then moves downward; it spreads over the body by the second day. After two to three days, it disappears.

Other

Before the rash appears, children may feel tired and may have a low fever. They develop swollen lymph nodes ("glands") on the back of the neck and often experience joint pain.

WHEN to CALL YOUR CHILD'S DOCTOR

Call immediately if:

- Listlessness or convulsion.

WHAT YOU CAN DO

Keep your child comfortable and make certain that he/she has no contact with anyone who may be pregnant.

Review immunization records on your other children.

VISITING YOUR CHILD'S DOCTOR

Visits are rarely needed unless possible complications exist.

RASH—SCABIES

Scabies is an irritation caused by mites. It is spread from person to person.

WHAT to LOOK for

Scabies produces small, red bumps often associated with burrows (itchy red streaks on the skin where the mites burrow). The bumps itch severely, and scratching them may make it difficult to distinguish the burrows. Areas that are commonly involved include the wrists, elbows, navel, genitalia, back of the hands and between the fingers. The head and neck are rarely involved. Infection may develop with crusting or weeping lesions.

WHEN to CALL YOUR CHILD'S DOCTOR

Call within a few hours if:

- Scabies suspected;
- Red, tender, crusting or weeping lesion.

WHAT YOU CAN DO

Specific medicines kill the scabies mite. Apply Kwell lotion to dry skin from the neck down and leave for eight hours. Then, totally remove the lotion, usually by bathing the child. Eurax cream can also be used, applying the cream once, repeating it in 24 hours and then bathing your child. Children may continue to itch for as long as one week after a successful treatment.

Treat all household members (unless pregnant). Wash linens and clothes that have been used recently by the infected child. Put away linens and other items that are difficult to wash for at least four days.

Use antihistamines, such as Benadryl, for severe itching.

VISITING YOUR CHILD'S DOCTOR

Your doctor will confirm the diagnosis and prescribe the appropriate medication.

CAUTION

▼ Do not use Kwell if there is any question of pregnancy in the family.

RASH—SCARLET FEVER

Scarlet fever describes the combination of rash, fever and sore throat associated with a streptococcal infection (Group A).

WHAT to LOOK for

Rash

Small, red bumps are present, and the skin feels like sandpaper. Usually the area around the mouth is pale, and skin creases are pronounced. The rash lasts about five to seven days and then peels.

Other

Sore throat, swollen lymph nodes, headache, fever, and abdominal pain may all occur.

WHEN to CALL YOUR CHILD'S DOCTOR

Call within a few hours if:

- Small, red bumps; sandpapery skin; pale mouth area; pronounced skin creases;
- Sore throat, fever, swollen lymph nodes, headache or belly pain.

WHAT YOU CAN DO

Scarlet fever is no more serious than any strep throat. In the older child, throat lozenges or hard candy, especially butterscotch, are soothing to the throat. Use honey for young children over one year old. Acetaminophen is good for relieving pain. Some children respond well to gargling warm water.

Your doctor will prescribe antibiotics. Give as indicated until the entire prescription is taken. Children are contagious for 24 hours after starting the medicine.

VISITING YOUR DOCTOR

After doing a complete examination to confirm the diagnosis, your physician will usually do a throat culture and prescribe medicine to treat the infection. Sometimes your doctor will do a throat culture at the end of treatment.

SORE THROAT

Sore throats are common in children, often with other complaints related to a streptococcal or viral infection.

WHAT to LOOK for

Sore throats often cause painful swallowing with fever, big lymph nodes ("glands") in the neck, headache and belly pain. Your child may complain of difficulty eating and swallowing or be resistant to drinking and eating.

Streptococcal infections are difficult to differentiate from viral infections without a throat culture but more commonly have associated fever, white pus on the tonsils, tender and enlarged lymph nodes and marked difficulty swallowing. Streptococcal infections may also cause a sandpapery fine rash (scarlet fever) with accentuation of the creases at joints.

More serious infections produce a painful throat. Rarely, they may cause drooling or marked difficulty with swallowing, breathing or moving the jaw. "Fever" or canker sores produce pain on swallowing as do dental cavities.

WHEN to CALL YOUR CHILD'S DOCTOR

Call immediately if:

- Severe difficulty swallowing;
- Difficulty breathing or any drooling;
- Pain or limitation of jaw movement;
- Extreme pain.

Call within a few hours (culture usually indicated) if:

- Fever, white pus on tonsils, tender lymph nodes or sandpapery fine rash;
- Belly pain;
- Headache.

Call for an appointment if:

- Exposure to streptococcus at home or school with any symptoms at present;
- Frequent sore throats;
- Sore throat present over 48 hours.

WHAT YOU CAN DO

Before starting home treatment, arrange for your child to see your doctor if indicated. Home treatment in older children may include throat lozenges or hard candy, especially butterscotch, to soothe the throat. Use honey for children over one year old. Acetaminophen (Tylenol, Tempra, etc.) is good for relieving the pain. Some children respond well to gargling with warm water.

VISITING YOUR CHILD'S DOCTOR

Your doctor will usually do a 24-hour streptococcal culture (quick tests in the office are often available) if your child has symptoms that may be caused by a strep infection. Cultures are not necessary for exposed but healthy children.

If your child's culture is positive, your doctor will start antibiotics. Usually your child will feel better in one to two days. Give the medicines as directed for the entire 10-day course; not finishing the total treatment can cause kidney or heart irritation. Children are contagious for 24 hours after starting treatment but may return to school or day care after this period.

If the culture is negative, discontinue antibiotics and discard them.

CAUTION

▼ The toxic (extremely ill) child with a painful or prolonged sore throat needs evaluation.

SUDDEN INFANT DEATH SYNDROME

Sudden infant death syndrome (SIDS) is a devastating event whereby a child dies unexpectedly of an unexplained cause. Although children up to one year old may suffer SIDS, the majority of deaths occur between two and four months of age. Many SIDS victims have recently had a cold, cough, fever, vomiting or diarrhea.

Although it is poorly understood what causes SIDS, it is probably related to some relative blockage of the airway, which prevents adequate breathing.

WHAT to LOOK for

Commonly, children will experience a near-SIDS episode, whereby they briefly stop breathing but then quickly resume, often in response to your early resuscitative efforts. Immediate help can save these children. Begin CPR immediately. If SIDS has taken place, your child will not be breathing and his/her heart will not be beating. Immediate action is required to restore lung and heart activity. Begin CPR immediately (See page 106).

WHEN to CALL YOUR CHILD'S DOCTOR

Call immediately (Call 911):

- In all cases or if your child is not breathing.

WHAT YOU CAN DO

Begin life support for your children as described on page 106. Children who have had a near-SIDS episode can be resuscitated. Guidelines for immediate action are outlined in Ch. 7; your actions must be aggressive and directed toward the lungs and heart.

Arrange immediate transfer to the nearest emergency center.

VISITING YOUR CHILD'S DOCTOR

To provide optimal care, your child will be taken to the nearest emergency department. Steps to support your child's airway will often have been completed; early assessment will focus on deciding how much potential injury has occurred.

If full resuscitation is indicated, the hospital staff will mobilize its resources and initiate a number of procedures. You will see a host of physicians and assistants working toward one goal—saving your child.

TESTICULAR PAIN

Twisting (torsion) of the testicle stops the blood supply and causes damage to the testicle.

WHAT to LOOK for

Testicular pain may occur suddenly, causing intense lower abdominal and testicular pain. This is an emergency situation. The scrotum is swollen and the testicle is exquisitely tender. Nausea and vomiting may occur. Trauma may have preceded these symptoms.

Less serious problems can also cause pain but are usually milder and less rapid in onset. Infection of the testicle or epididymis can cause pain, but is usually slow in onset. Only a part of the testicle is tender, and the pain is not excruciating. Direct injury to the testicle also may occur. Hernias cause pain in this region as well.

WHEN to CALL YOUR CHILD'S DOCTOR

Call immediately if:

- Sudden, intense testicular pain;
- Trauma to testicle with subsequent pain;
- Mass that is swollen, blue or tender.

Call within a few hours if:

- Worsening testicular pain;
- Discharge from penis.

WHAT YOU CAN DO

In general, testicular pain requires immediate evaluation by your physician.

VISITING YOUR CHILD'S DOCTOR

The examination of the testicles and scrotum will assist in determining the problem. Special tests are available if the problem is unclear. Often your doctor will consult a urologist.

CAUTION

▼ Rapid onset of scrotal or testicular pain requires immediate evaluation.

VOMITING

Gastroenteritis or "stomach flu" usually causes vomiting. Minimal spitting up or regurgitation may be normal in infants and decreases as your child gets older. It becomes a problem if it suddenly increases in amount or frequency.

WHAT to LOOK for

Vomiting is often accompanied by nausea, fever and diarrhea from either an irritation or an infection of the intestines. Changing the diet often improves this. Additional symptoms imply other problems. Watch for green, bloody or "coffee-ground" vomitus; swelling of the abdomen or marked changes in behavior.

Infections of the ear, urinary tract and brain can cause vomiting, usually without diarrhea. Accidental poisoning with lead or excessive aspirin can cause vomiting with blood. After a head injury, vomiting can occur immediately and become problematic if it continues. Vomiting after injury to the belly or swallowing a foreign body can mean there is some blockage.

Some neonates and infants spit up a great deal or vomit occasionally. *Chalasia* results from the muscle between the stomach and food pipe being too relaxed and allowing food from the stomach to come back into the mouth, often within 30 to 45 minutes of feeding. It is common in newborns; as long as your infant is doing well, it is an inconvenience rather than something to be concerned about.

Spitting up may also be caused by feeding problems and techniques.

Dehydration (loss of water) may develop.

WHEN to CALL YOUR CHILD'S DOCTOR

Call immediately if:

- Vomitus has blood;
- Severe or prolonged (more than two hours) abdominal pain;
- Belly or head injury;
- Poisoning;
- Possible foreign body;
- Behavioral changes causing irritability or listlessness;
- Dehydration with decreased urination, less moisture in diapers, no tears, rapid breathing, irritability or sleepiness.

Call within a few hours if:

- Vomiting for more than 24 hours;
- Vomiting without diarrhea;
- Child is routinely taking medications that may contribute to vomiting;
- Painful, frequent or bloody urination;
- Ear pain.

Call for an appointment if:

- Recurrent problem.

WHAT YOU CAN DO

Avoid solids for six to eight hours. Small feedings usually work, often starting with tablespoon amounts of clear liquids. These fluids may include Pedialyte or Lytren for the infant, popsicles, ice chips and room-temperature, defizzed soda in older children. Slowly increase the amount over six to eight hours. After this period without vomiting, slowly expand the diet to include toast, dry crackers, clear soup, broth, etc.

Infants with chalasia usually respond to careful attention to feeding techniques. Keep your child in an upright position during feeding. It is often helpful to keep your child upright in an infant chair during the 30 to 45 minutes following feeding. Feed your baby frequently with small amounts and burp often. Use formula or milk thickened with small amounts of dry cereal.

A foreign body in the intestines does not necessarily mean that there is a blockage. If no other problem exists and your doctor doesn't think the object is stuck, watch your child's stool for passage.

VISITING YOUR CHILD'S DOCTOR

Your doctor will evaluate your child for dehydration (loss of fluid). The history should help determine possible causes. Additional tests and specific treatment will reflect the suspected problem.

CAUTION

▼ Vomiting without diarrhea or following trauma or ingestion requires evaluation.

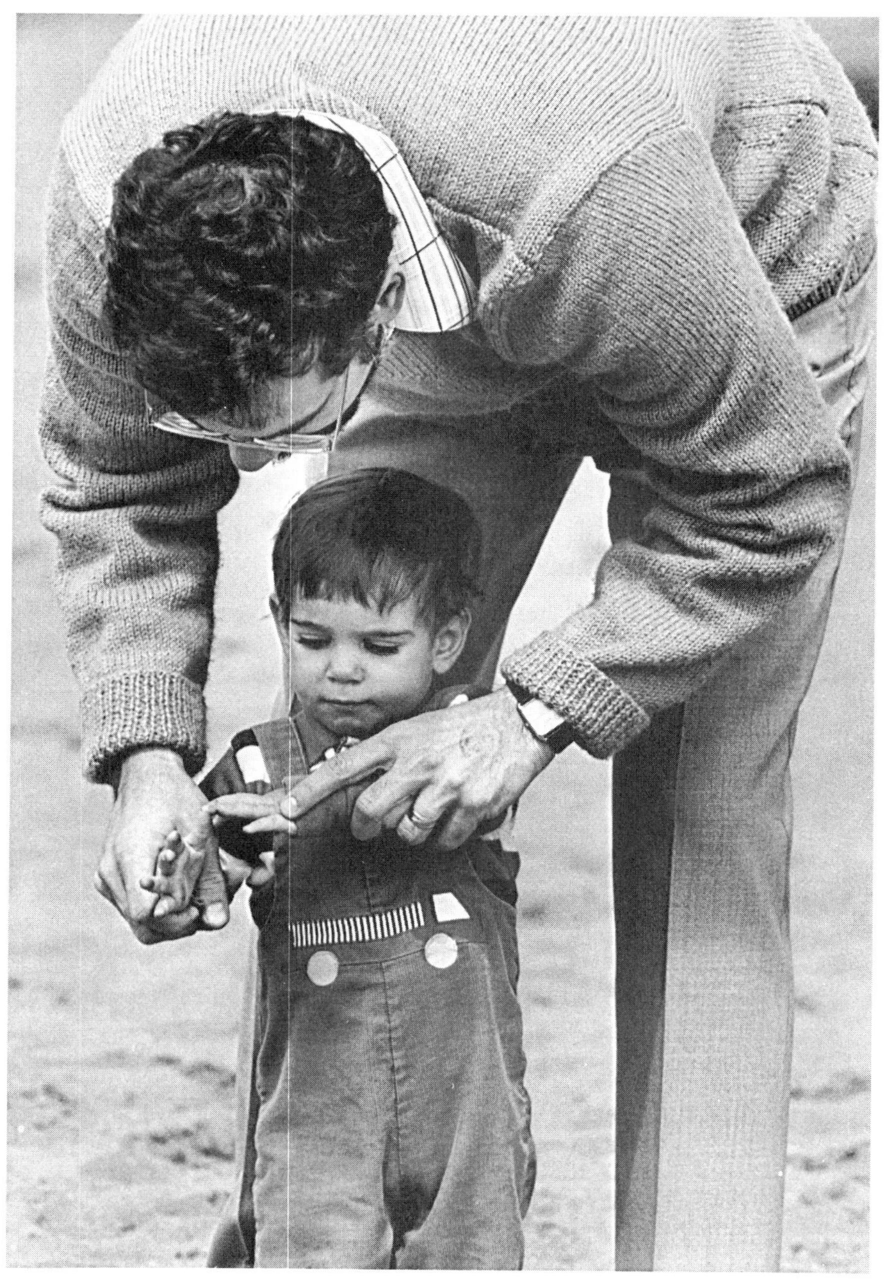

IF YOUR CHILD IS INJURED

Chapter 9

Your child can be injured in a variety of ways. Minor injuries usually involve scrapes and bruises and an occasional broken bone from sports or normal play. Such injuries are inevitable as your children explore their world and develop increasing independence. More serious injuries occur when children are involved with motor vehicle accidents, either as a pedestrian or a passenger.

Your doctor or nearby emergency department can usually care for small cuts, bruises and breaks. A careful examination, a thorough cleansing of the involved areas, and perhaps a few stitches (sutures) or a cast will be enough. Follow-up will usually be needed.

Serious injuries require immediate action, optimally in a setting that can care for all of your child's needs. Children often do not immediately show signs of the seriousness of their injury. Accidents in which there is a significant mechanism of injury involving a *major force,* such as an automobile, bicycle, other large object or a fall, require that your child see your doctor. Prolonged observation may be necessary.

If your child has an injury for which the explanation does not fit, explore other possible factors. Although unpleasant to consider, child abuse may be a contributing factor. The evaluation of children for abuse is designed to protect *all* children. Often the findings will show that the injury was accidental; the questioning process should be looked on as part of everyone's obligation to be certain that all children are well cared for and protected.

Injured children are often terrified and hysterical from pain and the strange and frightening environment. Reassure your child and be calm, even if on the inside you are also scared. Touching is important; talking in a calm voice is essential. Stay with your child when appropriate. Explain what is being done and avoid surprises.

CHEST OR BELLY INJURIES

The chest and abdomen (belly) are injured in falls, motor vehicle accidents, fights, etc.

WHAT to LOOK for

A host of problems following an injury may produce pain in the chest or belly. Your child is usually frightened, which can make a good evaluation difficult. Injuries may cause rapid pulse or breathing, severe pain, bleeding or bruising, dizziness (particularly if worse when standing up) or vomiting.

If the chest is involved, other symptoms may develop including difficult or rapid breathing; blueness of the skin, especially the lips and nail beds; unusual chest movements; or cough, often with blood. The pain may be in a specific area or it may be diffuse, involving the back or front.

Touching, moving or breathing deeply may increase belly or

abdominal discomfort. Vomiting may occur, often with blood, swelling or bruising of the abdomen, or blood coming from the urethral (bladder tube) opening.

Sometimes, children injure their genital region by jumping on a saw horse, railing or bicycle. Bleeding, extreme pain, swelling, discomfort and inability to urinate may develop. Be sure to exclude the possibility of abuse.

WHEN to CALL YOUR CHILD'S DOCTOR

Call immediately if:

- Accident with a major force, large fall or motor vehicle;
- Rapid pulse or breathing, dizziness, or bleeding;
- Severe pain;
- Difficult breathing, blueness of the skin, unusual chest movement or a new cough;
- Vomiting, swelling of abdomen or blood from the bladder tube.

Call within a few hours if:

- Pain;
- Inability to urinate, or bleeding, extreme pain, swelling or discomfort in genital area;
- Mechanism does not explain injury.

WHAT YOU CAN DO

Initially, keep your child calm and quickly attempt to determine what hurts, how much and what other problems exist. Then, **call for help** and arrange for rapid transport.

VISITING YOUR CHILD'S DOCTOR

Commonly, your doctor does an evaluation in an emergency department where facilities are available for a complete evaluation. The history of the accident and the physical examination will help determine what potential problems may develop.

Blood tests, urine analysis, X-rays, etc., may verify that there are no serious injuries. If an injury exists, your doctor can then take specific measures. If no problems are found, your child may be watched for a period to make sure that nothing has been overlooked.

CAUTION

- All children with problems following injuries to the chest or abdomen should be evaluated;
- Children may have multiple injuries.

CUTS AND SCRAPES

Cuts and scrapes are common for children and usually involve only a minor, superficial injury.

WHAT to LOOK for

Often, cuts and scratches only need to be cleansed and washed; at other times, they need stitching (suturing) and additional treatment. Look for the following in determining if medical treatment is needed:

Depth of the wound
The depth of the wound determines the involvement of internal structures such as muscles, tendons, blood vessels and nerves. Injury that is limited to the skin and fatty tissue beneath may require only cleansing and suturing; injury to other tissues requires repair before suturing.

Puncture wounds are difficult to evaluate; those on the extremities rarely cause much deep injury. Active bleeding, numbness or a foreign body left in the wound will probably need exploration.

Size of the wound
Larger wounds usually require suturing to hold the edges together and to minimize scarring. Abrasions and scratches usually require cleansing.

Location of the wound

It is important to minimize scarring following cuts and abrasions on the face. Stitching the face is more time consuming and requires more meticulous care than other areas. Wounds on the hands or feet often involve deeper structures, while other areas, such as the genital region, are difficult to care for without training.

Mechanism of injury

Accidents involving motor vehicles or those suggesting the possibility of bad injuries to many parts of the body demand a full examination of your child.

If your child's arm is caught in a wringer-like device, the injury may appear minor on the surface but may involve significant injury to the arm tissues.

If a body part such as a finger or toe is accidentally amputated, place it in a clean plastic bag and place the bag in iced water. If no bag is available, place the body part in a clean cloth. Do not immerse in water or ice directly.

Poorly explained injuries may indicate abuse. They require evaluation.

Electrical or chemical injuries require medical assessment.

Tetanus status

Children require immunization for protection from tetanus. Children with a major injury who have completed their initial shot schedule need an additional immunization if it has been more than five years since their last tetanus shot. Children with a minor injury need an additional immunization if it has been more than 10 years since their last tetanus shot. Obviously if they are behind on immunizations, this may be a good opportunity to update tetanus shots.

Infection

After several days, wounds may become infected, developing warmth, redness and tenderness around the area, and occasionally draining pus. Any infection should be seen by your child's doctor.

WHEN to CALL YOUR CHILD'S DOCTOR

Call immediately if:

- Possibility of major injury from a motor vehicle or other worrisome mechanism;
- Bleeding despite continuous pressure;
- Deep or large cut;
- Possible involvement of muscle, tendon, nerve or blood vessel;
- Cut on face or hand;
- Redness, tenderness, warmth or pus around wound;
- Wringer-type or unexplained injury;
- Cut or abrasion on head with any change in behavior or state of alertness.

Call within a few hours if:

- Minor cut with skin split open, i.e., needs sutures;
- Abrasion on face, hand, feet, genital region or large area;
- Any question about the need for tetanus immunization.

WHAT YOU CAN DO

Initially, put direct pressure on the wound for at least 15 minutes with a washcloth, towel or other cloth. If the initial dressing becomes soaked with blood, place additional dressings on the injury while maintaining pressure. Keep the injured area elevated at a level above the heart. After bleeding has stopped, wash the area with water (and soap, if available). Apply ice to the area to reduce swelling. Rinse well and be certain that there is no dirt, glass or other foreign material present.

Once bleeding has stopped, examine the wound more fully. If your doctor does not need to see it, make certain that it is clean. Any loose skin can be cut off with clean scissors. Wounds that appear to need professional evaluation should be seen without delay. If suturing is appropriate, your doctor will want to do it within several hours to reduce the risk of infection. After too long a period of time, suturing may not be possible.

If the cut is small, leave it exposed. Apply a nonstick dressing of gauze to a larger wound. Minor wounds that do not need sutures may benefit from bringing the edges together; do this by holding them together with "butterfly" bandages or by cutting a bandage or tape into small pieces to bridge the gap.

Soak puncture wounds in water and soap for a minimum of 10 to 15 minutes. These are not usually sutured. See your doctor for an in-depth evaluation if there is active, ongoing bleeding, numbness or pain.

Following the visit to your doctor, mild bleeding and discomfort may occur as the numbing medicine wears off. Follow specific instructions, but in general, keep the wound clean and dry for two days. You may wash it gently with soap and water. Dressings should generally be changed every day. If sutures have been placed, gently soak the area with water or peroxide one to two days before the sutures are to be removed to reduce scabs This may make removal of the sutures easier. Return to your doctor as directed to have sutures removed.

Special circumstances that may occasionally require a visit to your doctor:

Blood collections may occur **under the fingernail or toenail** after a finger or toe has been smashed with a hammer or other hard object. If the pain is severe, relieve it by making a hole in the fingernail. Open a paper clip and heat one end with a candle, cigarette lighter or fire. When the tip is red hot, touch it quickly to the nail and melt through the nail leaving a small hole and draining the blood.

If you cannot remove a **splinter under the nail** with tweezers, gradually shave the end of the nail until the splinter is exposed. Then remove it with tweezers.

Fishhooks can become embedded if your child's skin. Hook a thread around the curve of the hook. Push down on the hook's eye and shank to disengage the barb and then align the string with the long axis of the shank. Pull gently. If unsuccessful, the hook can be pushed all the way through and the barb cut off.

Remove a ring on a swollen finger by alternating five-minute intervals of soaking the finger in cold water and elevating it. Continue for a total of 30 minutes. Apply oil (mineral or cooking) to the finger. Another approach is to place a string under the ring and wrap it in loops around the finger from the end of the finger closest to the palm proceeding to the tip. The loops should be close and firm enough to depress and shrink the flesh. Pull the palm end of the string back toward the tip of the finger and tug slowly while pulling the ring off as the string unwinds. The ring may also be cut off with a ring cutter.

VISITING YOUR CHILD'S DOCTOR

Your doctor will examine your child to determine the extent of injury and the involvement of any internal structures. Then your doctor will use numbing medicine to reduce any discomfort before cleansing and reexploring the wound. If internal structures are injured, your doctor will repair them before suturing the skin.

Your child may require a tetanus immunization.

Often, your doctor may want to check the wound in a few days to be certain that it is healing well and that no infection develops.

Facial sutures will be removed in three to five days, while those in other areas will be left in longer.

CAUTION

▼ Your doctor should see any cut or scrape that may involve deeper tissues or may require suturing.

FACIAL INJURIES

A number of injuries may occur to the face including damage to the eyes or mouth.

WHAT to LOOK for

Eye injuries are common. Normal vision is a good indicator that the injury is probably not severe. Eye pain may occur from scratches on the eye surface. Blunt trauma with an object small enough to fit within the eye rim may cause blood in the front of the eye, often associated with a loss of vision.

Dental injuries occur from blows to the teeth from falls, sports or fights. Determine if the teeth involved are primary (baby) or permanent. Injuries can cause teeth to become tender, sensitive to cold or touch, loose, cracked, missing or displaced.

Bleeding can occur at the margin of the gums and the teeth. A dentist should see such problems immediately if a permanent tooth is involved and promptly if only primary teeth are injured.

Nose injuries are usually the result of falls or fights and just produce little more than a bloody nose. Substantial swelling, displacement of the nose or difficulty breathing through one or both nostrils may develop.

Mouth injuries are usually minor but may produce problems if not identified and cared for at an early stage. Small cuts on the inside of the mouth or on the tongue usually heal but may need suturing if they are large or deep. Children who fall with pencils or sticks in their mouths may puncture or otherwise injure internal structures and increase the risk of infection.

WHEN TO CALL YOUR CHILD'S DOCTOR

Call immediately if:

- Loss or blurring of vision;
- Blood in the front part of the eye;
- Injury to a permanent tooth;
- Difficulty breathing through one or both nostrils;
- Nosebleed continuing despite 10 minutes of continuous pressure.

Call within a few hours if:

- Eye pain;
- Injured primary tooth;
- Displacement of nose;
- Fall with a pencil or stick in the mouth;
- Explanation does not explain injury.

WHAT YOU CAN DO

Facial injuries often accompany other trauma. If there are other injuries, they are usually taken care of first. It is essential to make certain that the airway is clear and that breathing is adequate.

If there is an **eye injury**, check vision. If it is partially or totally impaired or there is eye pain, decide where to go for help. Patch the eye with a cloth or gauze until it can be examined to prevent further damage.

If a **tooth** is loose, try to reposition it with gentle pressure. Once in position, hold for five to 10 minutes. If a permanent tooth is lost, hold the tooth carefully by the crown (the part that is normally exposed) and wash gently with water to get rid of foreign material. Insert the tooth into the socket as soon as possible. If you cannot replace the tooth in its normal position, place the tooth under your child's or your tongue to bathe in saliva or place it in room-temperature milk while taking your child to the dentist. For a tooth to be successfully reimplanted, it should be done within one to two hours. The sooner the better!

Nosebleeds usually respond to compression of the soft and bony part of the nose, pressing downward toward the cheeks with the thumb and forefinger for a minimum of 10 minutes.

If there is a cut in the **mouth**, have your child rinse it. Encourage clear liquids over the next 12 hours. Ice or Popsicles may be useful.

If there is any evidence of **neck pain** or tenderness, try to lie your child down and keep his/her head still. Place your child on a board and tape the head facing straight up. Use filler material, such as towels or clothes on both sides of the head. Usually call emergency vehicles (911) to arrange transport to hospital.

VISITING YOUR CHILD'S DOCTOR

A careful examination will be done to exclude injuries elsewhere on the body, particularly involving the head and neck. If significant injuries to the head, neck, eyes or teeth are recognized, consultants will usually be asked for their help.

Evaluation and therapy will reflect your doctor's findings.

CAUTION

▼ Eye, tooth and mouth injuries should be dealt with promptly to avoid unnecessary complications. There may also be other injuries.

HEAD INJURY

Children are constantly bumping their heads or, less commonly, falling or being hit by some moving object. Usually no problems develop, but your child must be watched to be sure no complications develop.

WHAT to LOOK for

The circumstances of the accident are important. The type of injury is determined by whether the accident was the result of a direct blow from a strong force, a serious fall or an accident involving a moving vehicle. Children may lose consciousness immediately following such an injury or have a period of relatively normal behavior followed by problems. Following head trauma, children may have a loss of memory or be disoriented or dizzy. They may develop visual problems, vomiting, nausea, headache, neck pain or convulsions.

Determine immediately if your child has any neck pain.

WHEN TO CALL YOUR CHILD'S DOCTOR

Call immediately if:

- Injury involves a large force, a serious fall or a motor vehicle;
- Decreased consciousness immediately or soon thereafter. Does not know name, date, location;
- Irregular breathing or pulse;
- Loss of consciousness for more than five seconds;
- Increased sleepiness or drowsiness, or inability to waken patient from sleep;
- Change in equality of pupils (i.e., the black centers of the eyes become unequal in size), blurred vision, peculiar movements of the eyes or difficulty in focusing;
- Stumbling, unusual weakness, problem using arms or legs, or change in normal gait or crawl;
- Personality or behavior change, such as increasing irritability, confusion, restlessness or inability to concentrate;

- Persistent vomiting (more than three times);
- Blood or fluid drainage from nose or ears;
- Black eyes or bruising behind ears immediately following injury;
- Convulsions or seizures;
- Neck pain;
- Large cut, persistent bleeding or deformity of head.

Call within a few hours if:

- Cut requiring suturing but without other problems;
- Headache worsening;
- Explanation does not adequately explain injury.

WHAT YOU CAN DO

Make certain that your child's breathing is adequate and that no other problems exist. Place a cold cloth on the point of impact to reduce swelling. Watch your child for changes in behavior or alertness for at least a day following the accident. Examine your child every two to four hours to be certain that he/she is improving. Continue to monitor the pupils (black spot in the center of the eye), level of consciousness and communication skills. Awaken as necessary.

Wash and clean any cuts and scrapes after bleeding has stopped. Large or deep cuts may need stitches.

Give aspirin or acetaminophen for pain. Stronger medicines will not usually be given because of the importance of watching your child's behavior and alertness over the next day.

Limit activities and restrict to a light diet.

If there is neck pain or tenderness, don't allow your child to move around. Gently position your hands on the sides of his/her head until you can place your child carefully on a board and tape the head facing straight up from the board. Use filler material (such as towels or clothes) on either side of the head to keep it from moving. Arrange for ambulance transport to the hospital.

VISITING YOUR CHILD'S DOCTOR

Your doctor will take a history and do a careful physical examination that includes the entire body as well as the head. If there is any pain or discomfort when the doctor moves or touches your child's head, X-rays will be ordered. Most children, however, will have no worrisome symptoms and will be able to go home. They will need to be under careful supervision for at least 24 hours.

If your child is having problems, your doctor will suggest a period of observation in the hospital. A skull X-ray may be helpful, but more sophisticated approaches such as the CAT scan machine, which looks inside the skull for signs of injury, are used more widely. The results of this study as well as periodic reevaluations will determine any need for hospitalization.

CAUTION

▼ All patients with bad head injuries or worrisome findings need evaluation and observation.

▼ *All children with neck pain or tenderness following injury should have their head and neck restrained to prevent movement until the neck injury can be evaluated.*

SPRAINS AND BROKEN BONES

Children are frequently involved in accidents that produce pain, swelling and tenderness of their arms, legs, hands or feet. Although these accidents usually cause only bruises or sprains, broken bones can occur. The greater the force involved, the more likely there is to be a fracture. Children's bones are more easily injured than adults' but heal more rapidly.

WHAT to LOOK for

When trying to determine what kind of injuries there are, it helps to find out how the accident happened. The nature of the injury should conform to the mechanism.

Tenderness, swelling and bruising may be present over the painful area. On the basis of physical examination alone, it is very difficult to be certain that a bone is not broken. Particular problems may arise if the area is cold, blue or numb or looks deformed, with or without the bone exposed. Children are often unwilling to bear weight or make normal movements with an injured extremity.

WHEN TO CALL YOUR CHILD'S DOCTOR

Call immediately if:

- Limb or joint is deformed or shortened;
- Limb is cold, blue or numb;
- Extreme pain;
- Pelvis, hip or thigh is tender;
- Child is pale, sweaty or dizzy (may worsen when sits or stands);
- After casting is applied, severe pain or pressure within the cast, increasing blueness or coldness, excessive swelling or decreased motion of the fingers or toes that are involved.

Call within a few hours if:

- Unable to bear weight;
- Decreased use, movement or function of limb;
- Moderate pain;
- Marked swelling;
- Bleeding or laceration;
- Injury to elbow with marked swelling;
- Mechanism does not explain injury.

Call for an appointment if:

- Persistent pain beyond 48 hours;
- Reduced mobility of limb in days and weeks following injury.

WHAT YOU CAN DO

Apply ice to involved area and keep elevated to lessen pain and swelling. Gently touch to determine how much swelling, pain and deformity are present. Compare the injured area with the same region on the other limb. If there is bleeding, apply pressure.

In most cases, take your child for evaluation. It is often useful to explain to children what may happen. A brief discussion about X-rays may be reassuring. (There is no pain if they hold still; it's like taking a picture.) Arrange immediate assessment if there is a deformity or evidence of poor circulation (blue, cool or numb). Deformed limbs, especially if the bone is visible, should be moved as little as possible. Rolled-up magazines or newspapers may serve as a temporary splint. Splint the joints above and below the involved area.

If there is only a sprain, elevate the limb and apply ice packs for the first 24 hours. Rest is essential, although it is useful to wiggle the finger or toes periodically. An elastic bandage and crutches restrict movement and prevent weight bearing or use. Slings are useful for shoulder problems.

Keep the cast dry (unless a Fiberglas cast is used). Do not place foreign objects under the cast or pull the padding out. If there is severe pain or pressure within the cast, increasing coolness or blueness of the fingers or toes, or excessive swelling or decreased motion of the fingers or toes, your doctor may need to apply a new cast.

Once a cast or bandage is removed, your child will feel weak, but should gradually increase activity.

VISITING YOUR CHILD'S DOCTOR

Your doctor will determine the extent of the bone injury and if there is nerve or blood vessel damage. An X-ray will determine if there is a fracture. If there is no fracture, your doctor may recommend rest for the joint using a combination of elastic bandage, sling, crutches or splint.

Specific problems are very common in children:

Broken clavicle (collarbone) commonly occurs from falls or blows to the shoulder. Children may complain of pain over the collarbone and refuse to use their arm. A special splint ("figure of 8") keeps the shoulders straight. Collarbone fractures heal well.

Pulling an infant's arm may produce a **nursemaid's elbow.** The child will not use the arm because of pain at the elbow. If there are no complicating injuries, your doctor can reduce the pain by twisting the wrist so that the palm faces upward and then bending (flexing) the arm at the elbow. There is usually a click, and the child almost instantaneously begins to use the arm.

Knee sprains often occur during sporting events and may involve any one of a number of ligaments. These sprains may permit abnormally increased movement from side to side or from front to back. Or the knee may lock and not straighten. Sprains hurt immediately and usually continue to be painful, in contrast to the typical ligament tear, which is painful initially but resolves relatively rapidly.

Ankle sprains and fractures are very common, with the foot twisting either in or out. There is usually immediate pain and swelling. One place often hurts more than others when fractures are associated with springs.

CAUTION

- Since it is difficult to be certain that a bone is not fractured, it is usually wise to have the injury examined;
- Bone injuries may occur with other problems.

APPENDICES

APPENDIX A: GROWTH MEASUREMENT

As you monitor your child's growth, your doctor will measure weight (either in pounds or kilograms), height (either in inches or centimeters), and head size (either in inches or centimeters). These are important measures of how your child is doing physically. Charts, such as those in Figures 1 to 4, are useful for picturing your child's rate of growth. It is not as important to determine if he/she is taller or shorter than other children than to be certain that the growth rate is adequate.

You may want to plot your child's growth each time you return from your doctor. On the chart are percentile lines that denote the relative range of normal. For instance, if your child is at the 50 percent line for weight, that means that 50 percent of children are heavier and 50 percent are lighter. If the percentile is 20 percent for weight, that indicates that 20 percent of children are lighter and 80 percent are heavier. It is not important how much your child weighs or how tall he/she is, but that he/she is growing at the same rate as in the past. This is best determined by being certain that your child is growing along the same percentile curve on the charts. If you have a question or are concerned, you may want to review the charts with your physician.

Weight

Weight can be measured in pounds or kilograms; these measurements are easily convertible as noted in the following table.

In addition to monitoring your child's weight increase on the growth charts, a few interesting landmarks may be useful. Infants during the first month of life usually gain about one ounce or 30 grams per day after the first week of life. By five months of age, most children have doubled their birth weight. By a year, the weight will have tripled.

Weight conversion table (pounds and ounces to grams)

Oz.	0 lb.	1 lb.	2lb.	3 lb.	4 lb.	5 lb.	6 lb.	7 lb.	8 lb.	9 lb.
0		454	907	1361	1814	2268	2722	3175	3629	4081
1	28	482	936	1389	1843	2296	2750	3204	3657	4111
2	57	510	964	1418	1871	2325	2778	3232	3686	4139
3	85	539	992	1446	1899	2353	2807	3260	3714	4168
4	113	567	1020	1474	1928	2382	2835	3289	3742	4196
5	142	595	1049	1503	1956	2410	2863	3317	3771	4224
6	170	624	1077	1531	1984	2438	2892	3345	3799	4253
7	198	652	1106	1559	2013	2467	2920	3374	3827	4281
8	227	680	1134	1588	2041	2495	2948	3402	3855	4309
9	255	709	1162	1616	2070	2523	2977	3430	3884	4338
10	284	737	1191	1644	2098	2552	3005	3459	3912	4366
11	312	765	1219	1673	2126	2580	3034	3487	3940	4394
12	340	794	1247	1701	2155	2608	3062	3516	3969	4423
13	369	822	1276	1729	2183	2637	3090	3544	3997	4451
14	397	850	1304	1758	2211	2665	3119	3572	4026	4479
15	425	879	1332	1786	2240	2693	3147	3601	4054	4508

If patient weighs 10 pounds or more, the following are added to the value from the table above, to determine the final weight.

10 lb.	4.53 kg.	110 lb.	49.89 kg.
20 lb.	9.07 kg.	120 lb.	54.43 kg.
30 lb.	13.60 kg.	130 lb.	58.96 kg.
40 lb.	18.14 kg.	140 lb.	63.50 kg.
50 lb.	22.68 kg.	150 lb.	68.04 kg.
60 lb.	27.21 kg.	160 lb.	72.57 kg.
70 lb.	31.75 kg.	170 lg.	77.11 kg.
80 lb.	36.28 kg.	180 lb.	81.64 kg.
90 lb.	40.82 kg.	190 lb.	86.18 kg.
100 lb.	45.36 kg.	200 lb.	90.72 kg.

Length

Length is measured in inches or centimeters. One inch is equal to approximately 2.54 centimeters.

Children's length at birth is usually doubled by one year of age.

Figure 1
Percentile standards for growth: Boys birth to 24 months.

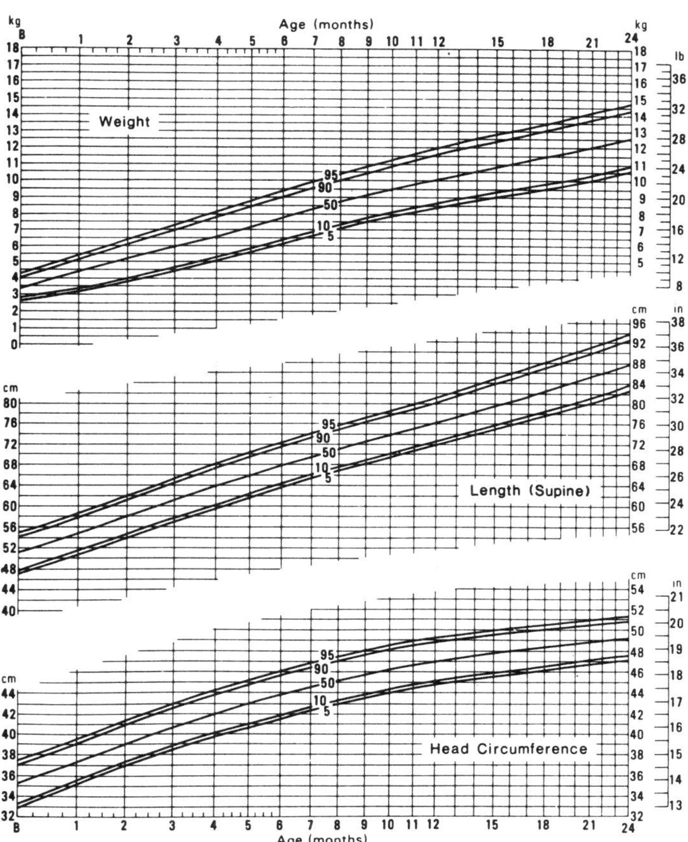

*Charts are modified from National Center for Health Statistics growth charts, 1976.

Figure 2
Percentile standards for growth: Boys 2 to 18 years.

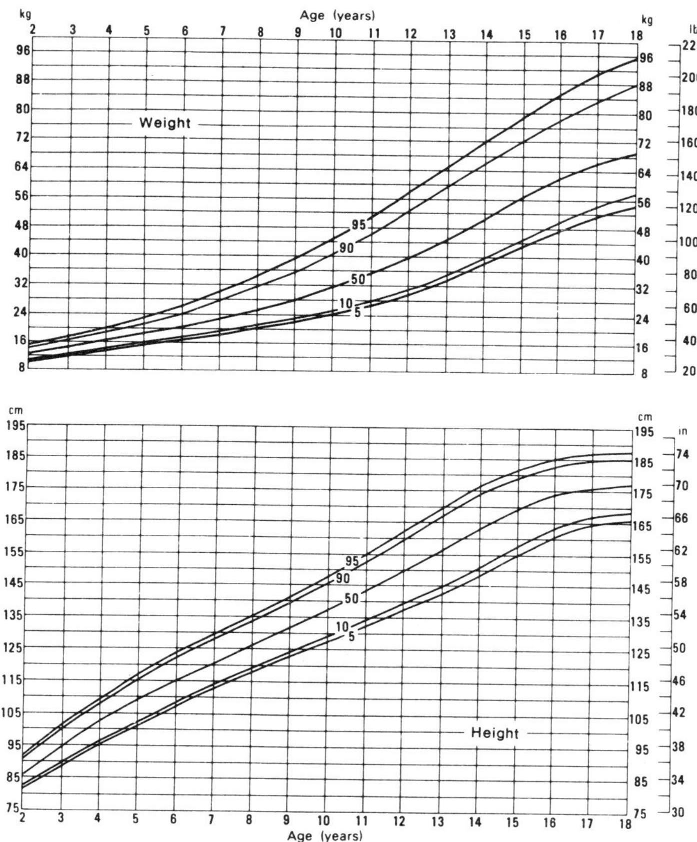

*Charts are modified from National Center for Health Statistics growth charts, 1976.

Figure 3
Percentile standards for growth: Girls birth to 24 months.

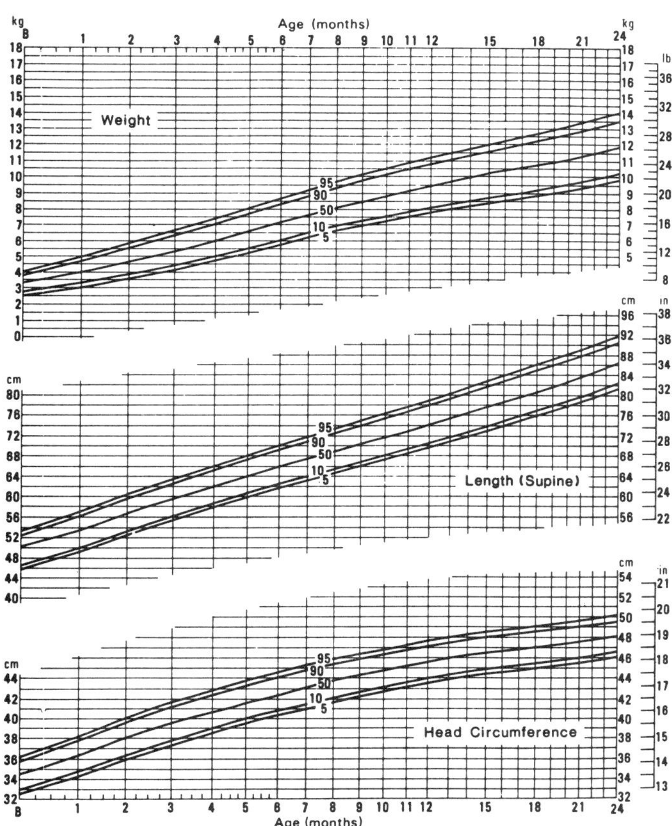

*Charts are modified from National Center for Health Statistics growth charts, 1976.

Figure 4
Percentile standards for growth: Girls 2 to 18 years.

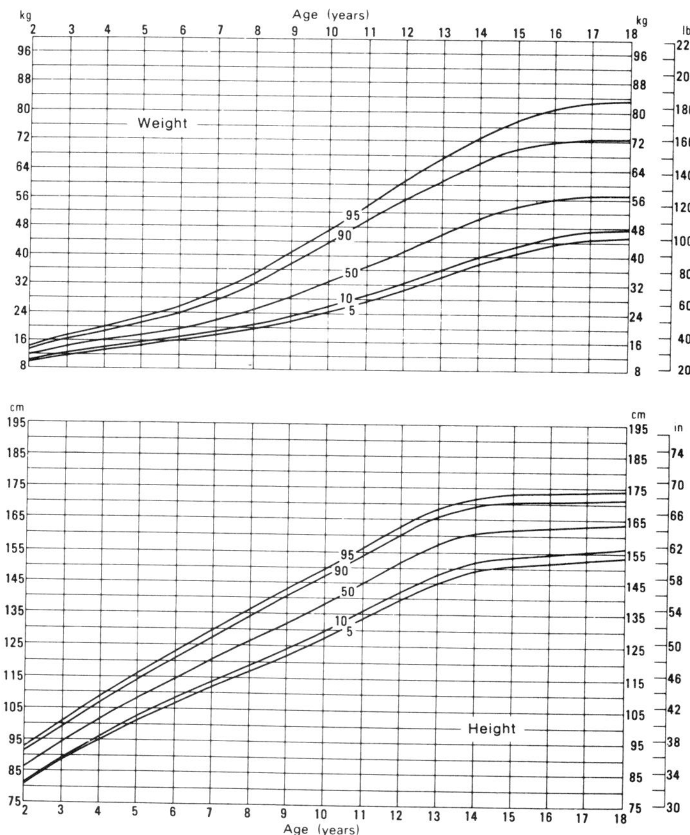

*Charts are modified from National Center for Health Statistics growth charts, 1976.

APPENDIX B: TEMPERATURE

Temperature is normally measured in either Fahrenheit or Centigrade. Either measurement system is correct and convertible. The table below summarizes this conversion. As a point of reference, a fever is usually considered to be a rectal temperature of 38° C or 100.4° F.

Centigrade (Celsius)	Fahrenheit	Centigrade (Celsius)	Fahrenheit
34.2	93.6	38.6	101.4
34.6	94.3	39.0	102.2
35.0	95.0	39.4	102.9
35.4	95.7	39.8	103.6
35.8	96.4	40.2	104.3
36.2	97.1	40.6	105.1
36.6	97.8	41.0	105.8
37.0	98.6	41.4	106.5
37.4	99.3	41.8	107.2
37.8	100.0	42.2	108.0
38.2	100.7	42.6	108.7

F° C°
Normal
98.6 37
100.4 38
Fever
102.2 39
104 40
105.8 41

APPENDIX C: YOUR BABY'S MEDICAL RECORDS

This section may be useful in organizing specific records about your child. You may want to note your child's weight, length, and head circumference on graphs in Appendix A. Keeping this information up to date will ultimately be time saving.

BIRTH HISTORY

Hospital ______________________________

Weight ____________________ Length ______________

Family doctor or obstetrician ______________

Apgar score: one minute ______________

five minutes ______________

Comments ______________________________

____

IMMUNIZATIONS

Vaccine	Date of administration					
	2 mo	4 mo	6 mo	18 mo	2 yr	4–5 yr
Diphtheria, Pertussis, Tetanus, (DTP)						
Oral Polio						
Measles, Mumps, Rubella, (MMR)						
Haemophilus influenza, (HIB)						

MEDICAL HISTORY

Date	Age	Hospital/ Physician	Problem	Comment

EMERGENCY INFORMATION

Your name ______________________________

Address ______________________________

Directions ______________________________

____

Phone Home ______________ Work ______________

Neighbor name ______________________________

Neightbor's phone ______________________________

Rescue squad phone ______________________________

(usually 911)

Your child's doctor ______________________________

Address ______________________________

Phone ______________________________

Nearest emergency department ______________________________

Poison-control center ______________________________

Pharmacy ______________________________

Child's medical problem(s) and comments

Child ______________________ Age ______________

____

____

Child ______________________ Age ______________

____

____

Child ______________________ Age ______________

____

____

INDEX

✦